Other books in the Jossey-Bass Nonprofit Sector Series:

SECRETS OF SUCCESSFUL
GRANTSMANSHIP

SECRETS OF SUCCESSFUL GRANTSMANSHIP

A Guerrilla Guide to Raising Money

Susan L. Golden

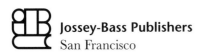
Jossey-Bass Publishers
San Francisco

Letter by Edward Skloot reprinted from the 1995 Annual Report of the Surdna Foundation, by permission of Edward Skloot.

Epigraph reprinted from GUERRILLA DATING TACTICS by Sharyn Wolf. Copyright © 1993 by Sharyn Wolf. Used by permission of Dutton Signet, a division of Penguin Books USA Inc.

Epigraphs from Mao Tse-tung, *Mao Tse-tung on Guerrilla Warfare*, reprinted by permission of The Nautical & Aviation Publishing Company, Second Printing, July 1992.

Epigraphs reprinted from GUERRILLA WARFARE, by Che Guevara, by permission of the University of Nebraska Press.

Epigraph reprinted from J.C. Wylie, Rear Admiral, USN, *Military Strategy: A General Theory of Power Control*, copyright © 1967 by Rutgers, The State University. Reprinted by permission of Rutgers University Press.

Epigraphs reprinted from GUERRILLA by CHARLES W. THAYER copyright © 1963 by Charles Wheeler Thayer. Reprinted by permission of HarperCollins Publishers, Inc.

Jossey-Bass Web address: http://www.josseybass.com

Manufactured in the United States of America on acid-free paper containing a minimum of 20 percent recycled fiber from postconsumer waste.

Library of Congress Cataloging-in-Publication Data

Golden, Susan L., date.
  Secrets of successful grantsmanship: a guerrilla guide to raising
money / Susan L. Golden. — 1st ed.
    p. cm. — (The Jossey-Bass nonprofit sector series)
  Includes bibliographical references and index.
  ISBN 0–7879–0306-X (acid-free paper)
  1. Proposal writing for grants. I. Title. II. Series.
HG177.G65 1997
658.15'224—dc21   96–45858

FIRST EDITION
PB Printing 10 9 8 7 6 5 4 3

THE JOSSEY-BASS NONPROFIT SECTOR SERIES

CONTENTS

Preface   xi

The Author   xix

Introduction: What They Don't Tell You in
    Grantsmanship Workshops   1

1   Know Your Territory: The Basic Principles of
    Guerrilla Grantsmanship   5

2   Where the Money Is: Conducting Effective Prospect Research   19

3   Opening the Right Doors   35

4   Making Your First Conversation Count   46

5   "Send Me Something in Writing": Documents That Get Results   57

6   Planning for a Successful Meeting (Before Submitting
    Your Proposal)   67

7   Preparing and Submitting Your Grant Proposal   78

8   Successful Meetings (After Submitting Your Proposal)   103

9   The Critical 25 Percent: Giving Your Request a
    Competitive Edge   114

Conclusion: The Guerrilla Grantseeker: Focused,
    Disciplined, Persistent   126

Resource A: The Foundation Center Directory of Free Funding
    Information Centers   129

Resource B: Budget Preparation Guidelines   149

Notes   161

Index   163

PREFACE

Translating ideas into reality almost always costs money, but people who have good ideas often lack the necessary funds. Grants are a good source of funding to make things happen, from starting projects to building buildings. Yet many people are reluctant to seek grants because they have become discouraged by their own fruitless efforts or intimidated by hearing about the failures of others. Some people employed in fundraising exacerbate these fears by promoting the myth that grantseeking is fraught with complexities that make professional help a necessity.

Genesis

I wrote this book to dispel the myths surrounding grantseeking and to show readers that they can become successful at it, either by themselves or by maximizing the use of professional help. The book is based on my twenty years of experience working with over 100 organizations of all types and my personal involvement in raising more than $700 million.

My goal is to help people avoid the waste of time and the anguish of failure I experienced before I figured out how the system works. I spent eight months in my first position as a development officer preparing proposals that were elegant, cogent, even compelling. I mailed them to appropriate foundations—ones that had expressed an interest in the kind of work we were doing—only to have my high hopes dashed as rejection letter after rejection letter came back in response. In despair, I apologized for wasting the organization's time and money, and offered to resign.

Fortunately, the enlightened people with whom I worked refused my resignation. Instead, the organization's chairman of the board got on the phone and started talking to grantmakers, and we then began a series of visits with them that opened serious dialogues. Nine months later the grant money started rolling in, and the rest, as they say, is history.

Need

Since then, competition for philanthropic funds has escalated dramatically, a trend that continues today. The field of fundraising has developed to the extent that the discipline now offers fully accredited academic programs devoted to the subject, as well as hundreds of books. Is yet another book really necessary? I believe so.

Despite the proliferation of instructional opportunities—from degree programs to countless workshops and short courses—and despite the barrage of books, pamphlets, and videos, most instruction on grantsmanship still is limited to the fine points of proposal preparation and some treatment of prospect research. What I have learned is that although good research is a *sine qua non* and good proposals are certainly necessary, in and of themselves they are not sufficient to generate grants. This book, therefore, offers a detailed explanation of the aspects of grantsmanship that *really* separate winners from losers. As relationships with grantmakers are the key to success in securing grants, I call this the *relationship model of grantseeking*; it focuses on establishing and building such profitable partnerships.

Purpose and Audience

If you have any level of interest in getting grants, this book is for you. Novice or seasoned professional, you will find it useful in your role as development officer, top executive, trustee, or manager in an organization; as a faculty member, student, or researcher; or simply as an individual who wants to get things done. If you are new to grantseeking, this book will take you step-by-step through the process. If you have been raising money for some time, you may find new insights, or at least descriptions of proven techniques articulated from a new perspective. You may find it handy as a one-stop reference for yourself or your less experienced subordinates. If you are teaching or taking a course in nonprofit management, you will find it a clearly written, practice-oriented text.

No matter what kind of work you do, this book may be useful. Grantseeking has much in common with selling or persuading in general. By substituting your interest for the word *grant* throughout the book, you can use it as a guide for convincing almost anybody of almost anything.

Scope and Treatment

In writing this book, I assumed that the reader might have no experience in persuasion, fundraising, or grantseeking. I include detailed, specific instructions on topics such as how to leave a message for a grantmaker and what to wear to a meeting with a foundation program officer. If these seem too elementary or trivial for you, please just skip over them; keep in mind, however, that they appear not only for the benefit of novices, but because over the years I have seen so many people—even well-educated, accomplished, sophisticated professionals—reduced to nervous wrecks by the challenge of grantseeking. My purpose is to reduce anxiety in grantseekers of any age or experience level.

After describing the fundamentals of the grantseeking interaction in the introduction and first chapter, I follow the grantseeking process in chronological order, from preparatory work through the advocacy that follows proposal submission. Throughout, I address the reader directly and provide explicit instructions about how best to conduct the dialogue on which relationships are built—relationships that will generate grants.

Each chapter focuses on a major task:

- Chapter Two: Conducting prospect research
- Chapter Three: Preparing for your first conversation
- Chapter Four: Conducting your first conversation
- Chapter Five: Preparing a preliminary document
- Chapter Six: Participating in a preliminary meeting
- Chapter Seven: Preparing your proposal
- Chapter Eight: Participating in a meeting after you submit your proposal
- Chapter Nine: Conducting advocacy activities to give your request a competitive edge

To my knowledge, this last chapter is a unique contribution to the literature. It may prove controversial, as I believe I am the first author either brave or foolish enough to foray into this territory. But because advocacy activities are critical to success in grantseeking, I felt I would be remiss to omit a discussion of them.

I conclude after the grantseeker has done everything humanly possible to obtain a favorable decision. I do not discuss subsequent relationships with grantmakers because such relationships can be maintained over the long term merely by continuously applying the basic principles upon which the relationship was initiated.

It may seem inconsistent that the longest chapter in this book is on proposal preparation, which I distinctly discount in its overall importance to the grantseeking process. Although the proposal alone is rarely sufficient to secure a grant, it is a necessary element in the process; the book would not be comprehensive without a detailed, step-by-step analysis of how good proposals are prepared. I give special and detailed attention to the preparation of the budget, providing an example and, in Resource B, a format you can use if the funder you approach does not provide something specific. The budget, I have learned, the section that many grantmakers scrutinize most carefully, is the area where many grantseekers do poorly, either underestimating resources required or not thinking through the details of project implementation.

You may be curious about or even troubled by the guerrilla metaphor used in this book. Although I chose it without a great deal of deep thought, I have determined to stick with it for two reasons.

First, upon reading the works of guerrilla warfare theorists, I was struck by how apt many of their observations are in regard to grantseeking. For instance, Che Guevara noted: "Generally guerrilla warfare starts from a well-considered act of will: some chief with prestige starts an uprising for the salvation of his people, beginning his work in difficult conditions in a foreign country."[1] So many of the projects I have worked on were designed "for the salvation of the people," and grantseekers often express the feeling that they are in a "foreign country." On a more mundane level, Mao Tse-tung once advised: "Before the meeting we must prepare for it. . . ."[2] Having seen the unhappy result of lack of adequate and appropriate preparation, I can't endorse this suggestion strongly enough, regardless of how I feel about the author's politics.

Second and even more important, I believe that the guerrilla metaphor makes a statement about the complexity of the relationship between grantseeker and grantmaker. To be sure, virtually every grantmaker—and many an expert grantseeker—talks about collaboration and fruitful partnerships between people on opposite sides of the desk. I myself believe staunchly in developing such relationships and in recruiting program officers to serve as a grantseeker's advocate. Nevertheless, underlying collaboration and intertwined with partnership is a strong adversarial element, just as there is in any dependent relationship.

This element, with its potential for abuse of power, is explored with great insight, candor, and balance by Edward Skloot, executive director of the Surdna Foundation, in his 1995 annual report:

> The relationship between grantmaker and grantseeker needs continuing attention and improvement, for theirs is truly an un-level playing field. Foundations have money. Nonprofits need money. Foundations control the timetable. Nonprofits control the word processor. Foundations establish the rules. Nonprofits deal with them. Paradoxically, in this ongoing, intricate relationship called the grantmaking process, both parties regularly feel misunderstood and frustrated.
>
> The vice-chairperson of the John D. and Catherine T. MacArthur Foundation, Elizabeth McCormack, perhaps the most respected philanthropic advisor in the country, recently told this story: She was asked by the executive director of a nonprofit on whose board she served to join her in visiting a foundation in order to present the case for funding. After having had the appointment canceled on a couple of occasions, the meeting finally took place. The two women were greeted by a young, unprepared program assistant who announced that the senior program officer was not available, nor anyone else, and that she would handle the meeting. That's not the end of the story.
>
> In the face of such treatment, neither of the visitors, and particularly Ms. McCormack, uttered a peep of complaint—then or later. It was difficult, even for the well-regarded and accomplished, to feel strong enough to convey to a funder how they really felt.
>
> The inconsiderate treatment of nonprofit staff is not the worst abuse of power. A more likely candidate surely is the "endlessly winding road." This occurs when foundations do not tell applicants where they stand in the grantmaking process, which can seem like an inscrutable black box that always has another hidden drawer. For many nonprofits, a quick "no" to a proposal is probably better than an excruciatingly slow "maybe."
>
> Equally troublesome is the case where foundation staff members know far less than the applicant's representatives. At few points in the process is simmering contempt more apparent than when nonprofit staff feel caught in a relationship they don't understand, governed by foundation officers who know substantively less than they do.
>
> Not all the problems lie at the feet of foundations. Numerous nonprofits are unbudgingly convinced that they have the answer. Even if they did, they still might not be appropriate candidates for funding. Grantmakers have their program priorities, defined guidelines, limited dollars and fixed timetables. On

occasion, too, a grantseeker's communications are garbled and its responses to the questions asked by the foundation are inadequate.

Thus, even under the best of circumstances, the harmonics can be wrong. It is terribly easy to miss a beat, forget a conversation, misinterpret a phrase or make a sideways remark which turns out to be upsetting, counterproductive or both.

At Surdna we are aware of this dilemma and we are trying to do something about it. Our program staff has had field experience and knows what it is like to be "on the other side." Each feels the tenuous nature of the relationship and how it can easily rise and fall, often in the same day or week. Each knows, too, how fortunate s/he is to have a job which, on a day-to-day basis, is certainly less stressful than his/her counterpart at the nonprofit organization.

My purpose in writing this book is to reduce the stress to which Skloot refers, a stress you probably know all too well. My goal is to provide enough details of the grantseeking process so that you can step back and view it in its proper perspective: as merely one component in the financial infrastructure needed to support your programmatic work. Through mastery of the skills outlined here, you will gain a sense of confidence and know that, regardless of the fate of any specific request, if your work has merit you will eventually find the support you need.

I wish you success in your grantseeking efforts and in all the important activities that will be supported through the grants you obtain.

Acknowledgments

Writing a book out of one's experience involves the contributions of many people.

First, I am indebted to my mother, Fay Bauer Landau, and my father, the late Irving L. Landau, for instilling in me a love of words and respect for the power of language.

I also wish to convey my loving gratitude to my sister, Marcia Landau Elbrand, who critically read and edited not only this manuscript but every major document I've composed since second grade.

I wish to thank my colleague Joseph R. Mixer for suggesting to Alan Shrader of Jossey-Bass Publishers that I might "have a book inside me." And my thanks to Alan for believing Joe, for encouraging me, and for waiting patiently throughout the long gestation of this project.

Whenever I got discouraged in the writing process, my friend Frederick E. Bryson kept assuring me it was worthwhile, and always gave me good directions.

My colleague and friend Laurence G. Mackie provided invaluable support and unflappable calm in the face of any computer problem.

I am grateful for the generosity of my dear friend Patricia Pasqual, director of the Foundation Center Library.

I am deeply indebted to my mentor, Joan G. Sugarman, who taught me that first and foremost, a proposal is a story.

I appreciate the perspective of Joanne K. Kaufman, who introduced me to the wacky world of federal grants and the rewards of entrepreneurship.

It was a privilege to work with Mrs. Frank E. Joseph, extraordinary volunteer fundraiser at the Cleveland Institute of Music. Her indomitable strength and courage inspired me.

My sincerest thanks to the clients who granted me permission to share their stories with you:

- Mary Brigid, executive director, Cleveland Rape Crisis Center
- Harriet S. Fader, executive director, Diabetes Association of Greater Cleveland
- Dr. Alice Kethley, executive director, Benjamin Rose Institute
- Kenneth W. McLaughlin, president, YMCA of Cleveland
- August N. Napoli Jr., president, Catholic Charities Corporation
- Dr. Michael J. Salkind, president, Ohio Aerospace Institute
- David A. Simpson, executive director, Hospice of the Western Reserve
- Gayle Doucette, executive director, Center for the Prevention of Domestic Violence
- Susan Janssen, executive director, Cleveland Eye Bank

And, of course, I owe enduring thanks to the nonprofit executives in over 100 organizations—people who began as clients and became friends through our work together and who have given me the privilege of participating in their dreams. They are all wonderful people doing important work, and collectively they have made it possible for me to learn about this fascinating field.

October 1996   Susan L. Golden
Cleveland, Ohio

This book is dedicated to
Donald, who made it necessary;
Marty, who made it possible;
and Joanna, Judith, Richard, and David,
who make everything worthwhile.

THE AUTHOR

Susan L. Golden is a consultant who helps organizations with capital campaigns and grantseeking. She has helped raise more than $700 million for projects in health care, education, social services, materials science, economic development, and the arts. She has worked with over 100 organizations, most of them in northeastern Ohio. She was recently honored to be selected Outstanding Fund-Raising Executive for 1996 by the National Society of Fund-Raising Executives Greater Clevland Chapter.

Golden began her career as a college English instructor, founding the Writing Lab at Cleveland State University and later the Developmental Education Program at Dyke College in Cleveland. She entered the field of fundraising as director of development at the Cleveland Institute of Music, where she worked for seven years.

Her education includes doctorate and master of arts degrees from Duke University, where she was a National Defense Education Act Title IV Fellow, and a bachelor of arts degree *magna cum laude* from Case Western Reserve University, where she was elected to the Phi Beta Kappa Society as a junior.

As a volunteer, she serves as vice president of the National Society of Fund-Raising Executives (NSFRE) Greater Cleveland Chapter and a member of the Research Council of NSFRE nationally. She also serves as executive director of The Landau Foundation, and is a member of Grantmakers Forum. She recently joined the editorial board of the *Journal of Non-Profit and Voluntary Sector Marketing.*

A Cleveland native and booster, she has endured a 40-year-plus love-hate relationship with the piano, and she dotes shamelessly on her daughters and nephews.

SECRETS OF SUCCESSFUL GRANTSMANSHIP

INTRODUCTION:
WHAT THEY DON'T TELL YOU
IN GRANTSMANSHIP WORKSHOPS

Guerrilla soldiers are brave, scrappy troopers who owe their success to spotting uncon-ventional opportunities in out-of-the-way places and making the most of each one. They operate without formal guidelines, flashy uniforms, or a reliance on safety in numbers.

SHARYN WOLF, *GUERRILLA DATING TACTICS*

If you're involved in a nonprofit organization today, one of your greatest con-cerns is probably maintaining your solvency. Whether you're the CEO of a struggling social service agency, a trustee of a community hospital trying to cope with changing reimbursement patterns, a rocket scientist seeking research money, an orchestra administrator awash in red ink, or a college president looking for ways to maintain enrollment, you know that survival can't be taken for granted. Some-times it feels like you're fighting a war, with no end in sight.

How do you fight the "red menace" of deficit operation that threatens so many nonprofits? You can reduce expenses, if you can do so without compro-mising the quality of your services. Or you can generate more earned income.

Another possibility is to find more philanthropic support. Unfortunately, as we all know, fundraising is a highly competitive arena; in some ways, it really is a jungle out there. When it comes to philanthropy, most people involved with non-profits think of direct mail, benefit events, and annual fundraising campaigns. Grants are also a way of improving an organization's financial situation, but seek-ing them is a very different process from mounting an annual fund appeal.

Most fundraising campaigns are organized like traditional military opera-tions, with generals mapping out strategy and troops accepting assignments, mak-ing phone calls, and visiting prospects. Grantseeking, on the other hand, is more like guerrilla warfare. You operate alone, or with a small band of colleagues, largely on an *ad hoc* basis. You look for opportunities, calculate the odds of success, and marshal your resources in order to offset your inherent weakness in the situation.

Many view grantseeking as a numbers game: they figure if they send out enough proposals, some are bound to get funded. But unlike the lottery or the slot machine, winning grants is not really a matter of the odds. Some grant applicants—admittedly a small minority—consistently win. The purpose of this book is to explain how they do it. As we will see, the difference between winning grantseekers and losing grantseekers is how each perceives the grantseeking process and how they behave based on those perceptions.

The Relationship Model

I call the set of activities that leads to success the *relationship model* of grantseeking—and twenty years of experience tells me that those who follow it can expect to win about 90 percent of the time.

The secret (which is really no secret) is to concentrate on establishing and maintaining good relationships with grantmakers. The grantseeking approach taken by those who succeed and that taken by the vast majority who fail differs significantly in two ways.

First, the winners tend to perceive the grantseeking process as highly personal, as any process based on relationships naturally must be. Though people with little experience may think that winning a grant should be impersonal—that grantmakers should be persuaded solely on a proposal's merit and attention to detail—most successful grantseekers know otherwise. They have observed that grant awards follow more from ongoing dialogue between grantseeker and grantmaker than from proposals. Perhaps the most revolutionary message of this book is that proposals in and of themselves don't matter—except insofar as they document the agreement between grantmaker and grantseeker. Not that proposals containing weak or sloppily described ideas get funded very often, but the number of good ideas and beautifully written proposals is so many times greater than the number of grants available that strong ideas and good proposals are *necessary but not sufficient* to secure grant support.

Second, winners view the grantseeking process as continuous rather than as a series of largely disconnected events. Thus they work on their relationships with grantmakers continuously, keeping up a dialogue and regularly communicating about many issues—grant support being only one. Although there may be periods of intense activity followed by quieter intervals, the grantseeking process is ongoing, as in any other successful relationship.

Who Will Benefit from This Book?

Most people are intimidated by what they've heard about or experienced in grantseeking. If you have ever tried it, the effort probably went something like this:

A phone call or piece of mail alerted you to a new funding opportunity, setting off several intense days or weeks of proposal preparation to meet the deadline. Though you managed to complete the work on time and sent off your proposal to the indicated office building downtown, agency in the state capital, or mail drop in Washington, you might as well have thrown it down a bottomless pit, for all you hear back. So you waited. Finally, a brief letter of rejection arrived, but it gave no meaningful reason why you were turned down.

If you have had this experience, or if you are afraid you will, this book is for you. You have lots of company. Most grantseekers—80 to 95 percent of all applicants—are declined, even if their project is based on an excellent idea and the proposal is on time, well written, and cogently argued. The problem, in short, is not with the project or the proposal but rather with the approach to grantseeking. This book is also for those professionals and volunteers who have had some success in getting grants but want to deploy their resources more effectively and improve their rate of success.

Because so many people are new to fundraising and so few have become proficient in grantsmanship, I assume the reader of this book has no prior knowledge of the process. So please bear with me if, once in a while, a point seems obvious or self-evident. Quite often, a principle that "goes without saying" is precisely the one that actually needs to be emphasized; even experienced people can lose sight of the fundamentals from time to time.

Throughout the book, I use detailed examples from my own experience to show you how my relationship model plays out in real-life situations. Most of these stories involve organizations I have served as an independent fundraising consultant. Though these organizations happen to be based in Cleveland, Ohio, a community that has always been a leader and innovator in the world of philanthropy, they could as readily have taken place anywhere else. Despite regional variations in grantmaking, the principles and methods advocated here are based on universal aspects of human nature and may be used effectively anywhere American philanthropy is practiced.

Skills You Will Acquire

This book will equip you to identify and exploit promising grantseeking opportunities. I hope it will also give you the wisdom—if not the courage—to refuse to waste time on opportunities that hold little real promise.

The objective is to help you get better results by using guerrilla strategies—picking your spots, sizing up your chances, and bringing the proper resources to bear at the proper time and in the proper way. You will learn guidelines that have been developed through experience, using common sense and basic marketing strategies.

You will be able to adopt successful strategies without having to master any new jargon, high-tech equipment, or complicated procedures. And you will be able to do all this with only a handful of colleagues or coworkers—if not by yourself.

In the following chapters, we will look first at some of the fundamentals of grantseeking. Among other things, you will learn:

- Why it's best to view grantmakers as prospective customers
- Various ways of gaining access to grantmakers
- Basic scenarios involving grantseekers and grantmakers that vary according to the type of support you are seeking
- How to tell when a seeming opportunity is actually worth pursuing
- How to identify prospective partners in the grantseeking enterprise
- What kinds of information to have at your fingertips before initiating contact with grantmakers
- The grantseeking process in chronological order, from the first phone call until the grant is made, including these skills:
  - Writing effective letters, concept papers, and white papers
  - Planning, orchestrating, and conducting in-person meetings with grantmakers, from get-acquainted sessions to site visits
  - Communicating both explicit and implicit winning messages to grantmakers
  - Preparing winning proposals (even though these play only a supporting role in the process)
- How to orchestrate advocacy efforts after your proposal is submitted

Grantsmanship, of course, represents only a small part of the fundraising universe. Every organization should have a good annual giving program, which may include direct mail, telemarketing, and special events. Periodic capital or endowment campaigns are also important, and major gifts and planned giving provide for the long-term future of most organizations.

Frequently, however, some of the largest gifts to an organization come from grants, whether you happen to be in a campaign mode or not. As we will see, grantsmanship is frequently the best way to secure the "venture capital" required to launch a new organization or a new program. Grants can even be used to challenge other donors in an annual fund campaign. All the basic principles and techniques of successful grantsmanship have applications to other modes of fundraising.

Once you understand and accept the basic dynamics of the funding relationship and have mastered the skills necessary to carry out the various tasks, you will not only survive the grantseeking process, you will thrive. Your investment of time, energy, and resources will pay significant dividends in the advancement of your organization's work.

CHAPTER ONE

KNOW YOUR TERRITORY: THE BASIC PRINCIPLES OF GUERRILLA GRANTSMANSHIP

A guerrilla unit should be thoroughly familiar with the terrain of its region of action.

MAO TSE-TUNG, *BASIC TACTICS*

Before you embark on a journey into unfamiliar territory, it's always a good idea to study a map. Likewise, before you begin seeking grants you need to become familiar with the "lay of the land" and the basic modes of getting around in this area.

This chapter introduces the essential elements of guerrilla grantsmanship. We will address three key questions:

- How can I best relate to grantmakers?
- Who's calling the shots?
- How can I get to the grantmaker?

Equipped with this orientation, you will find it easier to implement the strategies described in later chapters.

Understanding the Funding Relationship

As a grantseeker, your greatest challenge is to develop a good relationship with your grantmaker. Calling this the *funding relationship* highlights the purpose of the alliance from your perspective.

On the surface, what you want from a funding relationship appears quite simple: financial support in the form of grants. But the tendency to concentrate on one's own needs is exactly the reason so few grantseekers are successful. In funding relationships, as in virtually all relationships, an altruistic strategy seems to work best. The more you concentrate on your partner's needs, the more likely it is that your own needs will be met.

Individual grantmakers have different needs at different times, but some needs and expectations are universal and constant, arising as they do from the basic dynamic of the funding relationship. If you understand this dynamic and conduct yourself in such a way that you meet the grantmaker's expectations, you stand a much better chance of getting what *you* want from the relationship. What is this basic dynamic? Simply that grantmakers are prospective customers, and they expect to be treated as such.

Five Customer Constituencies of Nonprofit Organizations

If you are like many nonprofit executives, you may not be accustomed to viewing grantmakers as your customers, but it is helpful to do so as you begin thinking about the relationship into which you are entering. Actually, in the course of your career you have probably been involved in meeting the needs of several customer constituencies; see Figure 1.1.

To help you develop the strategies you will use to meet the needs of grantmakers, let's look briefly at each of these constituencies: who they are, how they relate to the organization, and their primary needs as customers.

Mission-Related Customers

Mission-related customers are those who use the services of the organization, such as the students of a school, clients of a social service agency, audience of a performing arts organization, or patients of a hospital. They are your most important customer constituency, for without them your organization has no reason to exist.

As organizations and their mission-related customers vary widely, the needs of a specific group of customers will also vary. However, all of them want excellence in service and responsiveness to their needs.

The relationship between mission-related customers and the organization's staff is direct, concrete, and often intimate. For instance, the very lives of patients in a hospital are in the hands of hospital staff, and the future careers of students in a school may be strongly influenced by the teachers they encounter.

FIGURE 1.1. THE NONPROFIT'S CUSTOMER RELATIONSHIPS.

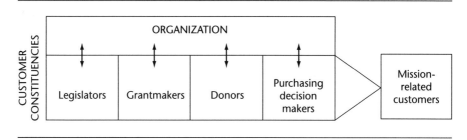

Although mission-related customers are essential to the nonprofit organization, they can never be its only constituency because they alone cannot keep it financially viable. Many nonprofits provide their services either for free, as in the case of a hunger center, or on a sliding scale, as in the case of a counseling service. Even if all clients pay the highest rate, the fees generated rarely cover the total costs, so the difference must be made up by others.

Purchasing Decision Makers

For some organizations, an important customer constituency is made up of *purchasing decision makers,* such as the parents who select schools and pay tuition for their children or the third-party payers who select health care providers and pay medical bills for patients.

The relationship between purchasing decision makers and the organization is less immediate and less concrete than in the case of mission-related customers. This relationship hinges on selection criteria and the values that drive the decision-making process. For insurers who select health care providers, for example, low cost is usually the highest priority; for parents of college-age children, the nature and quality of educational programming are the highest priorities, along with cost.

Once the selection is made, purchasing decision makers need the organization to deliver as promised so that they receive as few complaints as possible from the mission-related customers they represent. Purchasing decision makers can make it either easy or impossible for mission-related customers to use the service, and will do so based on whether the organization meets users' needs. Today's health care environment provides an extreme example: when nonprofit hospitals are unable to satisfy the needs of third-party payers, they may be acquired by for-profit chains or may even close their doors.

Donors

Another group of customers is made up of *donors*—those who make philanthropic gifts to the organization. These gifts may be used to reduce the gap between operating expenses and income, to implement new programs and services, to expand existing programs and services, to construct new physical facilities, or to expand, renovate, or equip existing facilities.

The relationship between donor and organization may be limited to the writing of a check, in which case it will be more abstract than the relationships with mission-related customers or purchasing decision makers. Many donors, however, are also current or former members of other constituencies. Some may be members of the governing board or other volunteer groups. In these cases, the relationship is clearly complex.

The needs of donors are as varied as the motivations that prompt them to give. The organization may meet a donor's need for recognition, for networking, or for social acceptance; other donors need confirmation that they are "doing the right thing" in terms of their personal philosophy or the values imparted by their families. On the highest level, an organization can help donors attain personal fulfillment or self-actualization through their acts of philanthropy, which do indeed provide enduring benefits to the community or society.[1]

For this discussion, individual donors are considered separately from grantmakers, who conduct their philanthropic activities through a foundation, corporation, or government agency. In the case of foundations established and controlled by individuals or families, however, the distinction may be a fine one, as we will see.

Legislators

The fourth group of customers is made up of *legislators*—elected officials who make the laws that dictate the form and amount of public support for nonprofit organizations. The relationship between legislators and specific nonprofits is more distant and abstract than any of the others we have discussed. Legislation deals with social outcomes, and nonprofits merely serve as an instrument to accomplish these outcomes.

For instance, the legislation that established Medicaid provides that medical care must be made available to poor people. When a hospital provides services reimbursed by Medicaid, it becomes, in effect, a government contractor that offers something promised by legislation and is compensated for it according to the terms of the law. The relationship between legislators and nonprofits, then, is defined by the legislation that authorizes the service and the appropriation to pay for it. What legislators want from this relationship is the assurance that the services provided are indeed those desired by their constituents, and that the constituents are satisfied with the services they receive.

Grantmakers: Your Fifth Customer Constituency

Now that we have examined four customer constituencies in a new light, you may be prepared to consider grantmakers as a fifth, whose needs require the same attention, resourcefulness, and intelligence you customarily employ to satisfy the needs of your other constituents.

In the grantseeking process, you will encounter several different types of grantmaking organizations. These may be staffed or unstaffed (that is, managed by paid professionals or simply by trustees); they may award grants on a local, state, regional, or national basis; and their assets may range from a few thousand dollars into the billions. Their interests are as varied as the realm of philanthropy itself— from animal welfare and civic beautification to medical research, education, and cultural advancement.

There are currently over 625,000 charities registered with the federal government, and the number is growing rapidly. For instance, in 1994, there were 599,745 registered charities, and by 1995, this number had risen to 626,226.[2] But according to the Foundation Center, there exist fewer than 11,000 foundations that give away $50,000 or more per year. As recently as 1992, foundations employed only slightly more than 6,000 professional staff, of whom about 30 percent worked for twelve of the largest national foundations.[3]

There are several kinds of foundations. *Individual* or *family foundations* are funded by contributions from individual benefactors or families who often exercise a high degree of influence, directly or indirectly, on the awarding of grants. Many of these foundations are established through a substantial bequest upon the death of the founder, which may later be augmented by contributions from other family members. The family foundation executive, if there is one, may be an attorney or other trusted family advisor who does the job part-time. At the other extreme, some family foundations built upon great private fortunes have grown into the world's most powerful grantmaking organizations, sometimes employing more professional staff than many of the nonprofits with whom they deal.

Corporate foundations are funded by major corporations, normally with annual contributions that vary with the company's profits. The foundation executive is usually a company employee who may have other responsibilities in public relations or community relations.

Community foundations are funded by contributions from numerous individuals and families in a given community, and limit their grantmaking activities to that community. Although grant awards are ultimately approved by the foundation board or its distribution committee, many donors retain a degree of discretion over awards made from the funds they contribute. Larger community foundations—such as The Cleveland Foundation, the first to be established—may employ several professional staff, including specialists in various areas.

Government agencies whose primary purpose is to make grants are funded by public contributions, generally through annual legislative appropriations. Prominent examples include the National Endowment for the Arts and the National Endowment for the Humanities, which operate specific programs through state councils of the arts and humanities. Most of these organizations are professionally managed and are advised by appointed boards of directors. In addition, government agencies at all levels—local, regional, state, and national—also operate *ad hoc* grantmaking programs mandated by current legislation. In working with these agencies, you may deal with an appointed board or an agency official; such agencies are valid prospects for a grantseeking effort.

Just as nonprofits do with their endowments, most individual, family, and community foundations invest the contributions they receive from donors in an attempt to maintain the integrity of donated funds. In other words, they invest the principal and use only the interest or earnings as the primary source of grant dollars. Whether the earnings are high or low, however, foundations are required by law to give away a specific small percentage of the endowment corpus each year.

To develop a sound funding relationship with grantmakers, three things are essential: first, acknowledge that they are prospective customers and behave with proper deference; second, have realistic expectations; and third, address the grantmaker's priorities and concerns.

Showing Deference to Grantmakers

Adopting the appropriate attitude of deference to grantmakers plays out in several ways. In scheduling meetings, for instance, both the place and time should be set at the convenience of the grantmaker; as the grantseeker, you should be the one to travel or shift other commitments to accommodate the grantmaker's schedule.

The topics of your conversation should also be determined largely by the grantmaker. You may choose to develop an agenda in advance of a meeting in order to ensure that your time together is used as efficiently as possible. But if the grantmaker wishes to discuss something else, that issue should become the focus of your attention.

The timing of a grant award is also up to the grantmaker. As a grantseeker, you would usually prefer to secure funding immediately, but most private foundations and government programs stipulate a specific deadline for the submission of proposals, a specific period during which proposals can be considered, and a specific date on which awards are announced.

If you approach a grantmaker who operates an ongoing program, there may be periodic submission deadlines, perhaps quarterly or annually. Consult your grantmaker about the best time to submit your application and follow the advice you receive. If the grantmaker is not willing or able to provide support until some future funding period, you will either need to delay your project's beginning or arrange for other funding sources in the meantime.

Most important, as in relationships with all customers, you should indicate your willingness—nay, eagerness—to anticipate what the grantmaker will want or need and provide it before you are even asked. If you are unable to anticipate her wants and needs, you should at least respond as promptly as possible once asked. When you study prospective customers and try to satisfy their wants and needs, it makes it possible for them to develop the trust and confidence in you that ultimately justifies their investments in your organization's work.

Operating with Realistic Expectations

In developing a sound funding relationship (or, once again, a sound relationship of any kind), it's important to operate on the basis of realistic expectations. In the past, you may have shied away from grantseeking because you heard about others' bad experiences. But rest assured that you can avoid most problems if you simply refrain from wishful thinking.

Everyone harbors an intense longing to be cared for and a deep desire for permanence. As a mature person, however, you probably accept that "living happily ever after" is the normal conclusion to events only in fairy tales and TV movies. You need to apply the same kind of realism to your grantseeking efforts. Confidence and high hopes must be tempered by the knowledge that *all* funding is *interim* funding—that the maximum duration of support from any source is a while, not forever. Thus grantseekers should always plan for life after the current grant terminates. Many grantseekers get into trouble because, deep down, they see the awarding of the grant as an end to their worries rather than as a milestone on a long road. Grantmakers, however, are generally clear and consistent in their communication: they insist that a grantseeker present a plan for supporting the project after the current funding runs out.

Problems arise when the grantseeker submits a plan for continued funding that is formulated specifically to *sound* reasonable to the grantmaker but that the organization cannot or does not wish to implement. If you are awarded a grant and do not pursue the plan for alternative funding, then you, your grantmaker, and everyone else involved will end up disappointed.

If you want to avoid this kind of heartache, look at the awarding of a grant as the initial step in the process, rather than the final step. Think of the period during which you will receive grant support not as a honeymoon, but as an opportunity to develop alternative sources of support. Focus on identifying and developing new revenue streams to support the activity during the next phase, if not on a continuing basis (see Figure 1.2).

Just as all funding is *interim* funding, all funding is *partial* funding. Dependency may work in some personal relationships, but it is counterproductive in a funding relationship. You may long to secure all the money you need for a project from a single funder, but grantmakers are generally put off by such a prospect.

Some foundations like to be part of a co-funding team, in which two or more grantmakers provide support, reinforce each other's judgment, and share the risk that the project may not work out. In other cases, an individual grantmaker may want to be the only *private* foundation to support a given project. No grantmaker, however, will likely want to be the sole source of support; each seeks assurance that you are building a diverse funding base, usually with a mix of sources of support. The most popular combination of support sources these days is the public-private partnership; another sound combination is foundation and individual support. In any case, when you meet with grantmakers, be prepared to reassure them by naming other prospective funding sources.

FIGURE 1.2. GRANT AWARDS LEAD TO ALTERNATIVE REVENUE.

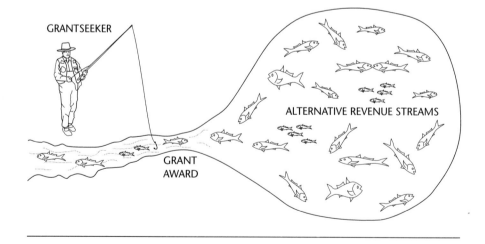

Addressing the Grantmaker's Priorities

As the vendor or supplier in a buyer's market, you want to emphasize your commitment to customer service in every way possible. As in other business relationships, you as grantseeker are well advised to frame your thinking and your presentation not from your perspective, but from that of your prospective partner, the grantmaker. Accordingly, you should do some research to determine what the grantmaker is looking for.

We will cover how to conduct this research in Chapter Two. But in general, though the agenda of each is unique, virtually all grantmakers are interested in advancing the mission of the grantmaking organization and in solving a specific problem (or addressing a specific opportunity) identified as a priority by the grantmaking organization. If you can demonstrate that your project will advance the funder's mission, or solve a problem identified by the funder, then your chances of success will increase geometrically.

But the most critical issues in a funding relationship are credibility and trust. Your grantmaker must know that you are who you say you are, and that you will do what you say you will. We will discuss ways of building credibility and trust later in the book, but first we must look more closely at the grantmakers themselves to understand where their authority is vested and how to gain access to them.

Who's Calling the Shots?

Salespeople evaluate customer potential by the size of the possible sale and the effort that will be required to make it. Grantseekers evaluate grantmaker potential by the size of the possible grant and the effort that will be required to get it. This will be explored in greater depth in the next chapter; for now let's examine the issue of authority, which influences both the size of the potential grant and the ease of persuasion. By and large, grantmakers hold one of two levels of authority, direct or indirect.

Direct authority is held by the person or persons who earned or inherited the money used to create a foundation. Grantmakers with direct authority enjoy the highest level of discretion over the distribution of funds and can make decisions about grants as quickly as they wish—even invading principal or giving away the entire corpus and dissolving the foundation to give an especially large grant if they are so motivated! Clearly, from the grantseeker's point of view the simplest and most expeditious option is to deal with a grantmaker who holds direct authority.

The grantmaker with *indirect authority*, on the other hand, merely represents or holds a proxy for those who have direct authority. In private philanthropy, the most common forms of proxy are family relationships and professional relationships. In the *family relationship*, a wealthy person designates a spouse, child, or another relative or relatives to be responsible for distributing grants. In the *professional relationship*, a wealthy person designates a trusted advisor such as an attorney, trust officer, or financial manager to distribute grants according to the wealthy person's wishes or the professional's best judgment.

In a professional relationship, grantmaking proxy authority is usually part of the terms of employment. This is typically the case in large private foundations and always the case in public agencies that make grants. In private foundations, the proxy represents the responsibility for making grants according to the guidelines established by those with higher authority; in public agencies, the proxy represents the public trust and carries with it responsibility for making grants that implement legislative intent. How much discretion or authority is held by the professional whose authority derives from a proxy? It varies widely, depending on how much confidence the people with direct authority have in the professional who holds the proxy.

The members of a grantmaking staff are usually hired as program officers, meaning they have authority over specific grantmaking programs. At most foundations, each program officer is responsible for a portfolio of requests. Some foundations give program officers responsibility for distributing specific funds.

Although it is preferable to solicit grantmakers with direct authority, that may be difficult or impossible. Such individuals tend to keep themselves remote from grantseekers socially, geographically, or both. Therefore, if you are like most of us, you must work with grantmakers whose authority derives from a proxy. As you forge alliances with them, it helps to remember the dynamics of the proxy situation, even though on a day-to-day operating basis most proxies are largely invisible. The distance between the donor and the individual holding the proxy may be considerable, but program officers usually have such a strong sense of responsibility for and control over their portfolios that they identify with the source of the funds they are distributing. They may even make statements like, "I'm not going to put any of *my* money into this." Such statements may strike you as arrogant or at least inaccurate, especially when the speaker is a government agent distributing taxpayer dollars or a community foundation officer distributing money donated by others.

But though such program officers didn't earn or inherit the money themselves, they do in fact represent those who did, and they are often largely responsible for deciding who will receive funding. For all intents and purposes, *they* are the customers and must be treated accordingly. The foundation's trustees, of course, have the final say on grant awards, but in most cases they merely ratify the recommendations of the professional staff. In a later chapter, we will discuss the delicate matter of marshaling any influence you may have with the trustees of grantmaking organizations.

In some cases, the authority of the proxy may be quite explicit. For example, the program officer may view your project as inconsistent with the values dictated by the absolute authority. At such times, you may hear something like this: "Although I *personally* see this project as having merit, I know that my board would not be interested." Because your request is being declined, such a statement may bring you little comfort. You can, however, use the program officer's declared personal interest as the basis for asking for help in identifying other prospective sources where your chances might be better.

How Can I Get to the Grantmaker?

How accessible is your grantmaker? It depends on the type of grantmaking organization and the individual's level of authority.

Program officers at most community foundations and government agencies are fairly accessible to most legitimate grantseekers. Busy program people may use screening or delaying tactics, such as requiring something in writing about a project before they agree to a meeting. Nonetheless, they will eventually agree to meet so long as the grantseeker can establish legitimacy by demonstrating that the organization she represents is eligible for a grant and that she has a specific project in mind that is appropriate for grant support.

In general, the higher the level of authority, the less available a person is. It can be fairly difficult for the average grantseeker to reach heads of federal agencies or trustees of national foundations. When the stakes are high and the competition is stiff, however, it may be worthwhile to spend some time and energy developing access to such individuals. This is a little-understood but critically important element of the grantseeking process. Methods of developing access depend on the sources of access—direct, indirect, or paid—you choose to utilize.

Direct Access

All access develops from situations where people come together and become acquainted. You probably have or could get access to more people than you think. A review of your potential sources of access may demonstrate that your network is large enough to do you some good.

As you think about the people to whom you have direct access, you can begin to identify those in a position to help you in the process. In general, the closer the relationship, the more good it can do you. There are times when the access provided by good friends is in itself sufficient to generate grant support. If the right person does the asking, the specific cause matters little as long as it falls somewhere within the grantmaker's purview.

Most of us have several potential sources of access to people: family, school, military service, and social, professional, and community activities. The circumstances of your birth provide you with access to an immediate family, and beyond this core group is an extended family brought about by births, marriages, divorces, and remarriages. So you frequently gain access to new people as they become relatives, or as children grow up and develop their own family networks.

From nursery school through graduate school, you had classmates—people with whom you shared significant experiences. If you went to boarding school, you may have gotten to know your classmates even better. In any event, if you made a phone call today to the person who sat next to you in tenth-grade geometry, you would probably get a fairly prompt response. Also during your school years, you probably were introduced to people through extracurricular activities. Sports teams, musical ensembles, school newspapers—all of these put you in contact with people who came to know you, likely remember you, and will at least listen to a request for help.

If you were in the military, people with whom you served usually remain accessible, having shared intimate and even life-changing experiences. If you served when the draft was still in effect, you may have met people who are now in a position to do you some good in civilian life.

Once you are out of school and the service, you meet people through social, professional, and community activities. As a working person, you probably meet and get to know people at all levels of your organization; through professional or business groups, you meet people working for other employers who have backgrounds, skills, and responsibilities similar to your own. As a community resident, you meet a wide variety of people, getting to know your neighbors just because they live nearby and making acquaintances at religious services, concerts, lectures, sporting events, and the like with people who share your interests and values. You get to know others because they share your life situations—other parents, other members of the same profession, even other people with the same disease or addiction.

No matter how reclusive a life you may think you lead, you probably come to the grantseeking table with a sizable network of people to whom you have direct access. In the next chapter we will explore how you go about identifying all the people you know who are involved in the grantmaking process. Meanwhile, you may still be concerned that among the circle of people to whom you have direct access, very few are in a position to assist you in your grantseeking efforts. This may indeed be the case. As a resourceful grantseeker, however, your access is not limited to people you know directly.

Indirect Access

You have indirect access to people who are known by people you know—friends of a friend, that is. Thus for everyone to whom you do have direct access, you have indirect access to several others. To determine in advance how much good an indirect introduction can do, you need to look at several factors:

- How close is your relationship with the person you want to act as your intermediary?
- How close is the relationship between your intermediary and the person (grantmaker) you want to meet?
- Does the grantmaker hold your intermediary in high regard? Will this association help to enhance your image? Will it help to establish you as a credible, trustworthy person?
- Does your intermediary have any influence with the grantmaker?

The answers to these questions will help you forecast how effective the introduction will be in positioning you with the grantmaker.

Paid Access

As in almost any other field of human endeavor, if you cannot identify a source of direct or indirect access to a grantmaker, you can pay for it. The kind of paid help you seek will depend on the funding source you want to approach. As we review each group of prospective funders—foundations, corporations, and government agencies—we will identify sources of paid access. For now, suffice it to say that regardless of financial concerns, it is generally better to use voluntary access than to pay for it. Volunteers simply have more credibility and influence than "hired guns." However, if the choice is paid access or no access, hiring someone might prove a wise investment. In grantseeking, as in any business enterprise, it takes money to make money.

Obviously, the person who is paid to introduce you has to be known to the grantmaker. In addition to providing an introduction, your intermediary should lay the groundwork for establishing a good relationship between you and your prospective customer. You can have the intermediary present your credentials, the true basis for your credibility. These include your education, professional experience, track record, and any kind of public recognition you have been accorded. Although none of this guarantees your credibility or trustworthiness, it does convey a sense of who you are and where you have been. That often brings a measure of comfort to the grantmaker, especially if the two of you have shared similar experiences. An increased comfort level makes a grantmaker more receptive to the idea that you could make a good partner.

The guerilla fighter needs full help from the people of the area. This is an indispensable condition.[4]

CHE GUEVARA, GUERRILLA WARFARE

CHAPTER TWO

WHERE THE MONEY IS: CONDUCTING EFFECTIVE PROSPECT RESEARCH

[Strategy is] a plan of action designed in order to achieve some end; a purpose together with a system of measures for its accomplishment.

REAR ADMIRAL JOSEPH C. WYLIE, *MILITARY STRATEGY: A GENERAL THEORY OF POWER CONTROL*

So far, we have reviewed the basic principles of guerrilla grantsmanship: viewing grantmakers as customers, showing them deference, and addressing their basic priorities and concerns, while always operating with realistic expectations and being able to demonstrate the financial support of others. We also noted that grantmakers have either direct or indirect authority to make grants, and that they may be approached by the grantseeker directly, indirectly, or through paid access.

Even this amount of knowledge probably gives you a significant tactical advantage over the other grantseekers with whom you compete. It is part of the proper mind-set needed to begin developing a strategy and preparing your approach to the grantmaker. But there is more to learn; getting ready to seek grants entails a comprehensive and intensive planning process. This and the following chapter outline the steps to take in developing the kind of relationships that lead to grant awards. They will allow you to understand in advance, before you pick up the phone to begin your first conversation with a future funding partner, several important considerations:

1. What type of transaction you are proposing to enter into
2. What kind of dynamics this transaction will involve
3. Who some of your possible funding partners are
4. Who can open the door, and how
5. What key facts you should present in your first encounter and which strategic approach is best

What Type of Transaction Will This Be?

As you embark on a grantseeking venture, ask yourself what type of transaction you hope to complete. There are two kinds, and most people new to grantseeking fail to reflect on the critical differences in dynamics, motivation, and strategies between the two.

In Scenario A, the most common type of transaction, the grantseeker initiates the contact and seeks support. Such situations include:

1. Development of a new project, service, or organization
2. Meeting an emergency need or completing a stalled project
3. Meeting an ongoing need

From now on, these will be referred to as Situations One, Two, and Three.

The other type of grantseeking transaction, Scenario B, occurs when the grantmaker initiates contact after identifying a problem or opportunity and deciding to invest in the area. The funder makes it known that a new source of support is available for those who offer solutions to the problem or ways to take advantage of the opportunity. In such cases, the grantseeker must decide whether it is wise to enter into a joint venture as defined by the grantmaker.

In both Scenarios A and B, the funder, who has the money, is more powerful than the grantseeker. However, the dynamics of the two kinds of deals are different, as are the opportunities available to the grantseeker.

If you are a Scenario A grantseeker, you think of the funder primarily as an avenue to securing the support you need or want. In building your case, you must rely on general information about the grantmaker's mission and demonstrate that fulfilling your need will also carry out that mission. Your position, however, is weak because you initiate the contact, build your case based on inferences about the grantmaker's interests that may or may not be accurate, and can clearly express only your own need.

You can strengthen your position by drawing the most accurate inferences possible and by emphasizing that support for your project will also benefit the funder. To the extent that you persuade the funder that you share certain goals and objectives, you come closer to a position of psychological parity or partnership; to the extent that you concentrate on your own need, your position grows weaker and you become a mere supplicant. For this and other reasons, get out of the habit of thinking, talking, and writing in terms of your organization's needs. You will be more effective if you focus on the needs of those you serve—your constituents, the community, and society. The difference is more than semantic; your organization exists not to solve its internal problems and perpetuate itself but to serve people.

Under Scenario B, on the other hand, responding to a funder's announcement of an opportunity can establish you as a potential partner with the funder, one that can help accomplish a task, solve a problem, or address a need. Successful grantseekers in such circumstances make the case that their projects will indeed accomplish the task, solve the problem, or address the need identified by the grantmaker. The goal is explicit, so you need not depend on inferences about it; and though the funder's financial resources make the deal viable, you are in the relatively strong position of being able to provide something she has publicly said she wants. As you are responding to a request, you are by no means a supplicant.

What Kind of Dynamics Will This Transaction Involve?

Once you have determined the kind of deal you are contemplating, you need to understand what dynamics are involved before you can develop an optimal strategy for success. Given the two scenarios and three situations defined above, here is an outline of the basic dynamics of each.

Scenario A: Organization Seeking Support

If you are seeking support for whatever reason, you are aware of a need and have in mind a way it can be met, and thus your goal is to identify a funder whose philanthropic or business purpose is compatible with supporting the activity you propose. Therefore, in making your approach, you must emphasize how this activity can help fulfill the funder's own mission. Discovering that mission is a matter of research: you may best be able to do it by reviewing previous grants the funder has made and speaking with the grantees about their projects.

Some of the strategic decisions you make will be determined by the situation—that is, the specific type of support you are seeking.

Situation One: Developing a New Project, Service, or Organization. This is the most common situation in which grantseekers pursue support. Perhaps, now and then, you have sat at the kitchen table late at night asking yourself, *"Wouldn't it be neat if we could . . . ?"* If so, your thoughts might be similar to those of nonprofit executives who asked themselves questions such as these:

- Wouldn't it be wonderful if parents of retarded children didn't have to worry about what might happen to their children after they die?

- Wouldn't it be great if welfare mothers had a network of friends, rather than being so isolated?
- Wouldn't it be a blessing to offer hospice care for families with terminally ill children?
- Wouldn't it be nice if inner-city kids could do something productive in the summer instead of hanging out and getting into trouble?

In reality, each of these questions did lead to the development of a new program or service, and in each case it was appropriate to seek external funding for the start-up costs. The nonprofit executives who asked themselves these questions sought support from funders with whom they already had established relationships, and they were all awarded grants.

Some problems can be addressed by developing a *project*, a specific set of activities to be accomplished within a specific period of time. More often, problems require the development of a *program*, a specific set of activities that will continue indefinitely but may require external funding only to get them started. In other cases, a project or program to counter a problem is already in place, but a new *service* may be necessary—that is, a new way to serve existing clients or a way to begin serving a new group of people. On occasion, a whole new *organization* may be needed when none exists to offer the services people need; this is fairly rare but does happen, as in the mid-1980s when AIDS was first diagnosed and patients and their families needed new forms of support.

Project, program, service, or organization: all have one-time start-up costs. Staff must be recruited and trained; facilities must be located and equipped; communications materials must be produced. And initial operating expenses must be funded until cash flow from other sources is sufficient.

Start-up costs are often the easiest kind of support to secure from philanthropic funders. Many foundation people consider themselves the venture capitalists of the nonprofit world, and by providing start-up support they can legitimately take credit for enabling a new enterprise to begin operation. Furthermore, if you are seeking start-up funding you usually have a strong position: you often will be perceived as bold, creative, and innovative.

Situation Two: Meeting an Emergency Need. Sometimes unanticipated events cause an emergency. Advance planning or insurance can safeguard organizations against many kinds of emergencies, but nonprofit executives may still be forced to make difficult choices that leave their organizations vulnerable. For instance, an organization whose income stream changes may find itself in a cash-flow crunch. If sound planning and effective fundraising programs are in place, the organization will have a cash reserve or an endowment fund that earns enough unrestricted income to meet the challenge. But just as many small businesses are undercapitalized, most nonprofits are underendowed and thus vulnerable to cash-flow crises.

Emergencies frequently have to do with capital needs: boilers blow up, roofs begin to leak, and so forth. Adequately funded and well-managed organizations set aside plant funds for such circumstances, but other organizations may be less well prepared. Individual projects are also vulnerable; good managers may start with sound plans and adequate resources, but unexpected conditions can change things. Building projects, for example, can be stalled by any number of conditions beyond one's immediate control—weather, labor problems, interruptions to income streams, unforeseen but necessary design changes. The need to complete a stalled project can constitute an organizational emergency.

For that matter, nonprofit executives may take risks that put the organization in a dangerous position. When the president of a college or the headmaster of a secondary school is forced to spend more than usual to recruit extraordinary talent, for example, faculty or scholarship funds may be depleted. If these funds are not promptly and fully replaced, the school may find itself short of critical resources down the road.

Whatever the circumstance, a single organizational emergency can have widespread ramifications and turn into a full-blown disaster. You may seek philanthropic support to meet the need, but the dynamics of this situation are very different from those involved in seeking support for a new project, service, or organization. Most critically, little benefit accrues to the funder who provides money to fix your roof or replenish your scholarship funds. To secure support in such a situation, you need to prove to your grantmaker that your organization has been neither incompetent nor imprudent. At the very least, you need to show that you have put into place strategies for staying out of trouble in the future.

Situation Three: Meeting an Ongoing Need. Although some activities undertaken by nonprofit organizations become self-sustaining, others never reach that desirable state. Ticket revenues, for example, may never provide all the funds necessary to mount a ballet or concert season. Client fees may never cover the cost of counseling the poor. Tuition alone will never pay the tab for higher education.

Many well-managed nonprofits try to compensate by adding revenue-generating ventures to their charitable programs, but rarely do these produce sufficient funds to balance the financial picture. So nonprofit executives often look to philanthropic sources for continuous support, even though most grantmakers prefer to make one-time or short-term commitments.

Some foundations, however, are sympathetic to certain causes, such as helping the poor or creating art. They understand that it is inherently difficult or impossible to manage such activities in a way that is profitable or even self-sustaining. If your organization fits this description, these are the kind of grantmakers to seek out.

Scenario B: Grantmaker Seeking Projects

When the grantmaker rather than the grantseeker wants to initiate a project, the dynamic of the relationship between the two is very different. For the foundation executive or legislator, the purpose is to address a problem by investing in experimental solutions. For the nonprofit executive, it is an opportunity to secure new money.

In this scenario, the key is to determine whether you have a realistic chance to compete successfully for an award. The most important factor here is the way you learn about the program. Foundations and government agencies generally announce new programs by disseminating a request for proposals (RFP) or a broad agency announcement (BAA). During the program planning process, well before these documents are issued, program officers usually have informal conversations about their plans with people they know and trust—often nonprofit executives who are current or former grantees. If you are among the people a funder calls to discuss a new program, you have already established a relationship with a high level of mutual trust and respect and are in an ideal position to submit a winning proposal.

Funders may also convene formal meetings of advisory groups to discuss the development of a new program. The people who participate in these learn about the opportunity first and may even contribute to the shape and details of the program. Again, if you are part of the planning process, it's very likely that any proposal you submit will receive funding.

Once the program concept is set, the funder distributes the RFP or BAA. Naturally, the only people who are on the mailing list are those with whom the funder has had some contact, and the nature and extent of your contact will determine to what degree your position is enhanced. If you once called an agency and asked to be put on the mailing list, that won't increase your chances of success much. On the other hand, if you are on the mailing list because you have received grants in the past, and your previous projects were successful, then your chances of succeeding again will be quite high.

The RFP or BAA often includes a notice of a public meeting or a series of workshops where representatives of the grantmaker will discuss the opportunity from the funder's point of view. If you attend such a meeting or workshop, you will have an opportunity to meet program staff and discuss the program (but not your specific project) with them. If this is your first meeting with the funder and you make a positive impression, it will increase your chances of winning an award.

By attending these meetings, you may learn that the project you have in mind has a low probability of being funded. Because it takes considerable time, energy, and resources to develop a full proposal, it is often worthwhile to learn enough to make a strategic decision *not* to submit one.

Invariably, many people who receive the RFP or BAA are unable to attend the workshops. Others receive the documents after the workshops have been held. If you don't attend a workshop, for whatever reason, your chances of winning an award will be dramatically reduced—not only because you have missed an opportunity to learn about the program but, even more important, because you have missed a major opportunity to meet and begin your relationship with the funder.

Many people read RFPs or BAAs only after hearing about them from others who are nice enough to share the news. But if you learn about a new program from a friend or colleague and you have no current relationship with the funder, your chances of winning an award are probably under 10 percent. You've gotten the news relatively late in the process, so you will have less time than many others to develop a relationship with the funder, and to work on a proposal before the deadline for submission.

Most nonprofit executives new to grantseeking have no idea what factors increase or decrease the likelihood of winning. They take the announcement at face value, becoming extremely enthusiastic and entertaining unrealistically high hopes. This may be natural, but to avoid later disappointment, the first thing to do when you learn of a new opportunity is to realistically assess the likelihood of winning based on the way you learned about it. If after doing so you honestly believe you have a reasonable shot at securing funding, then you need to answer the following three strategic questions to help determine whether the opportunity is really worth pursuing.

Is the Goal of the Funder's Program Compatible with the Mission of My Organization? Grantmakers usually state the program goal in the RFP or BAA, but not always in terms that help you make this assessment. If you are at all unclear about the funder's goal, call the funder and discuss it. This is a perfect opportunity to begin a relationship: asking a question that demonstrates that you understand the system and respect it.

If you determine that the funder's goal and your organization's mission are not compatible, do *not* submit a response no matter how tempting the prospect of bringing in new money may be. If you were to actually win an award in such a circumstance, you would have to implement the unsuitable project or refuse the funds. Either way, you create a problem for yourself.

On the other hand, your mission may be compatible with the funder's goals; if so, consider the following questions:

Is the Project You Have in Mind a Means to the Funder's Ends? To answer this question, you must make a distinction between means and ends. Many nonprofit executives new to grantseeking think that mounting a project is an end in itself, but that is not the case. To determine project ends, you need to step back and look at project outcomes—how the world will be different after your project is implemented. Then you must reflect on the ends sought by the funder and determine whether the two are compatible.[1] If they are, proceed to the following, final question in your preliminary assessment.

Do You Want to Enter into a Joint Venture with This Particular Funder? When you respond to an RFP or BAA, any funding you receive will become the glue that binds you to the funding organization. Accepting a grant represents a legal agreement to conduct the activities described in your proposal. So if you have any doubts about your plans, your intentions of following through on them, or your desire to enter into a long-term relationship with a particular funder, you need to face it early on—not after you receive an award.

Only if you can answer all three of the above questions in the affirmative should you proceed to develop your strategy, the first step of which is to conduct research to identify possible funding partners.

Who Are Some of Your Possible Funding Partners?

Finding funding partners requires both research and reflection. In grantseeking, part of your research will focus on locating people who can help you with this process.

Scenario A: Organization Seeking Support

Like many other activities, gathering information about funders is a matter of studying the three E's: elegance, ease, and economy. Elegance refers to the quality of the work, ease refers to the effort it requires, and economy refers to the cost. Because you must always choose between investing time and investing money, you can have two E's, but never all three. If you have more time than money, you can do it yourself. If you have more money than time, you can hire someone to do it for you. Elegance varies with the amount of time or money available.

Conducting Your Own Research. If you choose do-it-yourself research, one organization is a splendid resource: the Foundation Center. This nonprofit group collects published information about private sources of philanthropic funding and some information about public funding. It has national collections in New York City and Washington, D.C., regional collections in Cleveland, Atlanta, and San Francisco, and local collections in 190 libraries throughout the United States (see Resource A).

At the national and regional Foundation Center libraries, free orientation programs are available for new researchers, and Foundation Center staff members often visit local collections to conduct information sessions. Even if no video or personal orientation is available at your site, all Foundation Center collections have written materials that outline the research process and suggest places to start.

In Chicago, the Foundation Center is affiliated with the Donors Forum of Chicago Library, which is sponsored by a regional association of grantmakers in the Greater Chicago metropolitan area.

Working with Consultants. Just as you may pay for access to grantmakers if you can't identify sources of direct or indirect access, you may also pay for research. If you choose this option, you can hire either a research firm or an individual.

If you prefer a firm, in most locations you can select between nonprofit services and commercial ones. The most expert nonprofit service currently available is the Foundation Center. Its national headquarters employs five full-time researchers who will search computerized databases for a relatively modest fee. Some public libraries also offer fee-based research services. If available, as they are in most cities, commercial research firms can access national databases containing information about publicly held companies and their officers. Of course, to work cost-effectively with a research firm you must formulate your questions carefully. At the very least, you need to have a fairly clear idea of the kind of information you are seeking.

In working with research firms and computerized databases, the most serious limitation is the loss of the "serendipity factor;" computers ignore information that is proximate—connected by tenuous but potentially fruitful links. On hiring a research firm, interview the person who will actually conduct the research to make sure he understands your needs. Your researcher should be willing to take an occasional risk, and even to do some nonlinear thinking.

If you prefer to work with an individual, two national organizations can provide information about people in the fundraising profession: the National Society of Fund-Raising Executives (NSFRE), based in Arlington, Virginia, and the American Association of Fund-Raising Counsel (AAFRC) in New York City. NSFRE is the professional association for people involved in managing fundraising programs for nonprofit organizations. NSFRE currently has 125 local chapters and more than 17,000 members, and is still growing rapidly. The NSFRE Directory identifies those members who do at least some consulting work. AAFRC is the professional association of fundraising consulting firms. Most of these firms concentrate on providing counsel to organizations conducting major capital campaigns. Large consulting firms have little interest in grantseeking, as it is difficult to generate enough such business to keep their staffs busy and the fees generated are relatively modest. An AAFRC member firm, however, might be able to refer you to an independent consultant in your area who specializes in grantseeking.

A few words of caution: anyone can legally claim to be a fundraising consultant, and a few unscrupulous individuals periodically cause credibility problems for the entire profession. So be sure to exercise care in retaining the services of a consultant. Like other professions, such as accounting and financial planning, the fundraising profession has adopted a certification process. A professional who has met the standards administered by NSFRE is permitted to practice as a certified fundraising executive (CFRE); you might feel more confident if you select a consultant who has earned the CFRE designation.

Hiring somebody to conduct your research is like hiring anyone else: the clearer you are about your expectations, the more likely you are to get the results you want. But some nonprofit executives new to grantseeking think they can simply hire someone and instruct them to get grants. It won't work. No one can get grants for someone else, because grants come about through relationships between grantseekers and grantmakers. You can hire a consultant to fulfill some relationship functions, or to provide occasional interaction. But there is simply no substitute for a real relationship—that curiously complex, ongoing series of shared experiences.

Defining Your Needs. Whether you conduct your own research or retain someone to do it for you, it will be most productive if you begin with a clear idea of what you want or need. Just as novices may believe in the myth that they can hire someone to get grants for them, another form of wishful thinking is the belief that somewhere out there is a "magic list"—that if they can only identify the right foundation prospects through library research and send each a cogently written proposal, one or more checks will arrive by return post. And once in a great while, if a grantmaker is looking for new grantees or competition is light or the moon is in the right phase, this may actually happen. However, it doesn't happen much more frequently than a hole-in-one in golf or winning the lottery; don't count on it. It is far better to concentrate on identifying key individuals in the grantmaking process and developing relationships with them. Though this requires more time and dedication than merely developing a list and zipping off proposals, the investment of time and energy will pay off in the long run.

Where do you start? Two ways of doing research can lead more or less directly to identifying your best prospective funders. First, you can take advantage of the information readily available in your organization's records; and second, you can select those grantmakers whose mission and values most closely match those of your organization.

Reviewing your organization's internal records is the quicker of these two. Every nonprofit has a board of trustees, and most have a base of current donors, both large and small, which includes individuals, foundations, and corporations. Most organizations also maintain records of correspondence with foundations and corporations; from this you can learn who asked for previous grants and who was responsible for making them.

Depending on the type of organization you work for, you may also have records of individuals who benefited from or participated in your activities. Hospitals, for example, have physicians and grateful patients, and patients have relatives. Colleges have faculty, alumni, and parents. Social service agencies have clients, and clients have relatives. Presenters of performing arts programs have subscribers and audience members. In addition to the individuals currently affiliated with your organization, consider those who were affiliated in the past. There may be a reservoir of goodwill among family members of the people who were directly served. (There may also be reservoirs of ill will; if so, it's best to know about them.)

By going through all these institutional records, you can quickly and easily develop a list of people who know your organization and may be inclined to assist you with your grantseeking efforts. The other way to identify those who might help is to select grantmakers whose mission and publicly declared values match those of your organization. Consider the following factors as you put together a list of criteria for selecting these grantmakers.

Geographic Location. Location is almost as important in fundraising as in real estate. For most funders, it is the single most important criterion in awarding grants. Those in the private sector generally prefer to spend their money close to home. Individuals and families like to sponsor organizations in the community in which they live; corporations want to support organizations in the communities where they do business; and community foundations, by charter, support only organizations within a particular geographic area.

National foundations, on the other hand, usually try to distribute grants to all major regions of the country. They often strive to make awards to organizations that represent all kinds of communities, from densely populated urban centers to sparsely populated rural areas. Government funding also usually has a wider focus. The most common consideration in public funding is to distribute grant awards as equitably as possible throughout the political units (states or counties); less common is the targeted public program, in which grant funds are distributed to accomplish specific purposes in specific areas.

Although there is nothing you can do about your location, knowing the funder's geographic priorities can help you assess more realistically your odds of succeeding in a national or statewide competition.

Areas of Interest. It may seem obvious, but keep in mind the area in which your organization is working: health care, social services, the arts, and so forth. A program officer recently said that over half the proposals received by her foundation come from social service agencies, which her foundation does not support. Clearly, many grantseekers do not make sure there is a match between the work they do and the kind that the foundation or government agency supports. Sometimes, however, thinking about your organization's work in a creative way may help you identify more potential sources of support than you otherwise might consider.

When probing for matches with funders' areas of interest, research conducted by people rather than computers may well be superior, so doing it yourself may be more productive than hiring someone who is less familiar with your programs. If your project is relevant to several disciplines, it could attract a variety of funders.

True Story

The CEO of a social service agency with a preschool program became aware that many youngsters in his program were being abused at home. He wanted his staff members to be able to help the children and their parents stop the abuse. So the CEO and his staff developed a new project.

A child psychiatrist who specialized in dealing with abuse visited the center regularly. The psychiatrist met with and began treating the children in greatest distress. The psychiatrist also provided training sessions to raise the staff's awareness of child abuse, and taught laypersons strategies for dealing with these situations.

For this project, the social service agency was eligible to seek grants from funders with a variety of interests, including domestic violence, mental health, preschool children, families living in poverty, and education and training.

Thinking broadly and creatively about the area in which you are working may open new doors.

Type of Support. Most funders are very clear about the types of support they will provide. The basic categories are:

- Project funding—support for a clearly defined set of activities designed to accomplish a specific purpose within a specific time
- Endowment funding—financial assets that are to be invested to generate income; the income is expended and the principal remains intact

- Capital funding—investment in buildings, land, equipment, or anything else considered part of an organization's permanent physical assets
- Operating support—funding for ongoing expenses such as rent, utilities, and staff salaries
- Program funding—grants that reflect operating support if the program is ongoing, or project support if its duration is limited

Because most funders prefer to support projects rather than operations, grantseekers often go to great lengths trying to disguise operating needs as special projects. This is not a sound strategy, as any funder who's been around more than five minutes will easily see through it. It's better to use a straightforward approach: make a clear presentation of what you want or need, and proceed to develop the kind of relationship that can lead to the support you seek, even if it might not be immediately available because of the funder's published guidelines.

Range of Grants. The magnitude of the project or need is important in determining which prospects appear promising. In general, the larger the potential grant amount indicated by the funder, the better. Although it is unwise to put all your eggs in one basket, securing two or three large grants is clearly more efficient than going after dozens of small ones to raise the same amount of money. Remember that grants come out of relationships, and you will have to develop a relationship with each and every prospective funder you approach. Each will require time and attention.

People. Once you have selected funders that meet your criteria of location, area of interest, type of support, and range of grants, you can turn to the most important part of the research process: developing a list of individuals associated with the grantmaking organization. This is the heart of the grantseeking process!

Identifying key individuals is the most important part of any research effort, because your relationships with these people will ultimately determine your success. Your list of key individuals at each grantmaking establishment should include professional staff as well as officers and trustees. Exhibit 2.1 shows one format that many organizations find useful for identifying these relationships.

Reviewing such a list with the trustees or volunteers of your organization who are responsible for raising money can be very helpful. But as it is much easier to respond to a list than to generate one, you will identify many more contacts if you prepare a preliminary version, rather than generating it on the spot by asking your trustees to identify people they know who serve on foundation boards. Furthermore, if you do the review in a group, the dynamics of peer pressure will come into play, and people will be encouraged to sign up as solicitors.

EXHIBIT 2.1. FOUNDATION PROSPECTS FOR THE DIABETES ASSOCIATION OF GREATER CLEVELAND (DAGC).

Name of Foundation/Trustees	Relevant Recent Grants(s)	Suggested Request	DAGC Solicitor	Comments
BINGHAM FDN	$24,000 to	$25,000		
	Glynn-Brunswick			
Elizabeth Heffernan	Hospital to estab.			
Mary E. Gale	diabetes outpt.			
Thomas F. Allen	ed./treatment			
C. Bingham Blossom	program			
C. Perry Blossom				
Dudley S. Blossom				
Laurel Blossom				
Robin Blossom				
Benjamin Gale				
Thomas H. Gale				
Thomas V. Gale				
Laura Hitchcox Gilbertson, Staff				
F. J. O'NEILL				
CHARITABLE CORP.				
Hugh O'Neill	$15,000 to			
Nancy M. O'Neill	Alcoholism Services			
Rev. E. P. Joyce				
	$50,000 to CCF for			
*Applications not	Geriatric Ethics Program			
accepted—do we				
know anybody?	$100,000 to			
	Hitchcock Ctr.			
	See attached for more			
PRENTISS FDN				
Quentin Alexander	$1 M to St. Luke			
Richard A. Beeman				
Harry J. Bolwell	$390K to UH for Cancer			
Willam J. DeLancey				
J. Robert Killpack	$250,000 to CCF for Cancer			
Wm. A. Mattie				
	$20,000 to			
	Judson for A.D.			
	$400,000 to UH			
	for Ctr. Hum. Genetics			
	$150,000 to UH			
	for Cardiology			
	See attached for more			
REINBERGER FDN.				
Robert N. Reinberger	$100,000 to CCF			
William C. Reinberger	for neuroscience lab			
Sara R. Dyer				
Karen R. Hooser	$70,000 to Judson for AD			

As you conduct the review, be sure to ask your trustees to provide any information they can, whether or not they intend to contact the grantmaker themselves. For instance, if a trustee knows that a listed individual has the greatest influence on the foundation's decision-making process, it is essential for your organization to know that. If a trustee has information about the personal circumstances of any listed individuals, this can also be helpful in planning your approach. For instance, if a foundation trustee is nearing retirement or going through a divorce, this may affect his financial position or the chances of his responding to a request for special consideration.

Note and transfer to your organization's permanent file all the information gleaned from reviews. Foundation trustees generally serve for long periods, and the information may prove helpful for years to come.

Scenario B: Grantmaker Seeking Projects

When a funder announces an opportunity, the research strategies are different. To decide whether you want to respond to an RFP or BAA, you will need to determine the following:

- What kind of responses will be competitive
- What criteria will be used to separate winners from losers
- How stiff the competition will be

There are three sources of information who may be able to help: representatives of the grantmaker, colleagues who have more insight or experience than you, and consultants who specialize in grantseeking. In general, the closer your source to the grantmaker, the more valuable the information will be.

In evaluating information about a funding opportunity, two caveats are in order. First, be wary of colleagues who discourage you; those who are thinking about preparing a competing proposal are probably interested in reducing the competition.

Second, when considering government programs, bear in mind the appropriations game, played as follows: In Year One, an agency issues an RFP for a program funded at the $50 million level. The agency receives applications from 1,000 organizations requesting a total of $5 billion, but makes only ten grants averaging $5 million each. Lots of applicants are disappointed, but when appropriations time rolls around again the agency will be able to demonstrate sufficient interest in the program to justify an increase in its appropriation for Year Two. Legislators, interested generally in bringing more government dollars to their constituents and specifically in assuaging the feelings of those who were disappointed the first time, may be inclined to appropriate $100 million or more on the second go-round.

For these reasons, government program staff often encourage virtually every organization to prepare and submit a proposal. It's not because we live in a great democracy where every organization has an equal chance of securing public funds, but because staffers want their agency and its programs to appear important so the agency can grow and they can keep their jobs. And one way to demonstrate the importance of a program is to generate requests for many times more dollars than are available.

Most funding opportunities, public or private, are highly competitive. Don't waste your time developing a proposal if you see any indication that you might not stand a good chance of winning. You will be far more successful if you spend your time improving the odds by building relationships and then submitting proposals when you know your chances are good.

We should be informed of all aspects of the terrain that are disadvantageous to us . . . such as narrow roads, river crossings, circuitous routes for avoiding these river crossings and narrow roads, etc.

MAO TSE-TUNG, *BASIC TACTICS*

CHAPTER THREE

OPENING THE RIGHT DOORS

During the first stage, the [guerrillas] stress esoteric and exoteric appeals, as well as the social services and mutual help aspects associated with demonstrations of potency. One key objective at this time is the recruitment of local leaders. . . .

BARD E. O'NEILL, *THE ANALYSIS OF INSURGENCY*

In Chapter Two, we discussed the dynamics of two basic types of transactions: Scenario A, in which grantseeker approaches grantmaker in search of support for a project, and Scenario B, in which the grantmaker looks to fund projects that help solve a specific problem or achieve a specific purpose.

We noted that identifying potential funding partners under Scenario A can be done by conducting your own research or paying a firm or fundraising consultant to do it; evaluating potential partners includes considering such factors as their location and areas of interest, but in any case receiving a grant requires identifying individuals who influence the decisions of grantmakers. Under Scenario B, your research should focus on determining whether a proposal from you would stand a good chance of receiving an award.

Assuming you've done your research and identified one or more grantmakers worth approaching, it's time to move to the next step.

Who Can Open the Door—and How?

Again, the answer depends on the scenario.

Scenario A: Organization Seeking Support

Building new relationships is difficult and time-consuming, so it makes sense to approach those with whom you already have relationships before contacting others. Aside from pragmatism and efficiency, soliciting those nearest you first is imperative because they must demonstrate their faith in a project through their own financial support before other prospective donors will consider doing the same.

In addition to the members of your board of trustees, your organizational "extended family" includes current donors, volunteers, and employees, as well as mission-related customers—the people who benefit from the services you provide. "Friends" of your organization include former board members, past donors, and past users of your services. All these people already know and presumably like your organization, and you already have information about them that can help you identify those who might be the best prospects for a specific project.

One mistake nonprofit executives often make is neglecting to ask those closest to the organization for help. Board members have many fine attributes, but they aren't mind readers; the most common reason people give for not supporting an organization or project is simply that they haven't been asked. Your "friends and family" are often willing and able to provide the financial support you seek—*if they are asked*. As discussed in the next chapter, some of these individuals also may be very helpful in opening doors to other prospective donors, including grantmakers. Once they have made their own financial commitments, their credibility and influence with other prospects is greatly enhanced.

Board members sometimes try to direct the attention of nonprofit executives to large grantmakers, explaining that their own financial resources are limited or that they weren't brought on to the board to raise money. If this latter is the case, the responsibility lies with the executive who has avoided discussing fundraising with his board members. To be sure, not all board members have access to personal or corporate wealth, but each one can and should make some financial commitment to the work of the organization. Without that support, your chances of success with grantmakers are greatly diminished.

The first question that must be addressed is, how can you identify your best prospects? Other things being equal, it is always best to approach those who have the greatest financial capability, are closest to the organization, and have supported it most generously in the past. Beyond that, your selection of prospects will depend on the type of support you are seeking.

Situation One: Development of a New Project, Service, or Organization. When you are seeking this kind of support, reflect on two questions.

First, who has a natural interest? It makes basic marketing sense to match your new initiative with the interests of prospective donors. For example, if you're addressing problems associated with a certain disease, who among your constituents has had personal experience with the disease? If you're presenting an exhibit by a certain artist, who likes that artist's work? It is always easier for people to embrace a new idea when they are already interested in the general topic.

Second, what are the needs of the prospective donor? We naturally think of what our organization needs, but the donor also has needs, and perhaps these can be met by supporting the organization. For example, people who have lost loved ones to a disease may wish to spare others the same suffering. Or if a person is socially ambitious, he may long to be recognized by the members of the group he aspires to join.

People may be motivated by admiration, a desire to act on their values, a sense of obligation, or even guilt. The emotions and circumstances that cause donors to act are varied, complex, and sometimes unique. When we pay attention to donors' needs, we can choose the approach that will move them most deeply.

Situation Two: Meeting an Emergency Need. When faced with an organizational emergency, ask yourself three questions.

First, who is most likely to be sympathetic? Probably those who best understand how the emergency came about, and who perhaps participated in the decision that led to the emergency. Let's say, for example, that you are the school president and one year you overspent scholarship money to recruit a star quarterback. Next year, when you find yourself short of scholarship funds, approach first the people who encouraged you to do whatever was necessary to get the player.

Second, how urgently is the money needed? If your situation requires immediate action, you will need to approach a prospect who has the authority to write a check today. On the other hand, if your situation is already serious but won't reach crisis proportions until a year from now, you have some leeway.

Third, what is the magnitude of the need? If you need $100,000 immediately, you don't want to spend time on prospects who can give only $500 or $1,000. If you have no prospects capable of giving the full amount, seek a few gifts of $10,000 to $25,000.

Situation Three: Meeting an Ongoing Need. If your organization or project will always need philanthropic support, prepare reasonable answers for three questions.

First, why can't this enterprise break even? Answering this requires answering a few other questions as well: What is it about this undertaking that causes a financial imbalance? If your personnel costs are high, why do the people involved merit such compensation? If your clientele cannot afford the services, why do you want to continue serving them?

Second, what are some creative ideas for generating income beyond soliciting donors? Although fees-for-services may not be a viable approach to solvency, perhaps you could increase earned income through other means. Perhaps you could establish a gift shop related to your mission. Maybe some of your expert staff could provide some contract services as well as sliding-scale services.

Third, what kind of precedent is there for providing ongoing support? If you're in the arts, perhaps you want to remind people of the role of patrons since time immemorial. If you're in a field that until recently has been supported by public funds, maybe you need to remind voters that it was their preference to eliminate government support.

For any of the three situations, in soliciting help from an organization's "friends" or "family" the best approach is to see your most promising prospects personally rather than writing a letter or calling. A personal visit establishes the importance of the conversation and produces far better results. The ideal mode is the two-on-one meeting, with the staff person providing information and the appropriate volunteer (one who is known and respected by the prospect, and has already made his own commitment) doing the soliciting. The next best approach is a one-on-one visit by the volunteer. If no volunteer is available, then the professional must do the asking.

To those with little fundraising experience, it may appear more efficient to approach a group of people, rather than a series of individuals, but this rarely works well. When a group is solicited, each member can shrug off responsibility and assume another member will do what is necessary. When you speak to individuals, however, it's clear that the responsibility is their own.

The most effective two-person team to approach the "friends" or "family" of an organization is generally its CEO and its most respected and influential board member, often the chair. If you wish to work with another board member who has more influence than the chair, it is a good idea to inform the chair in advance to secure approval. Whichever volunteer will help you solicit funds, point out that the most effective fundraisers demonstrate their commitment to the project through their own financial support; in other words, make it clear that the volunteer is expected to get the ball rolling with a personal financial commitment.

Once that has happened, encourage the volunteer to take the lead in contacting the prospective donor; it is more difficult for the prospect to decline a meeting with a respected board member than to turn down a staff member. A direct approach is best. Urge your volunteer to let the prospect know up front that you want to talk about providing financial support for your project.

So far, we have discussed the best ways to open the door to the closest "friends and family" of an organization. But if you have secured all the support you can from these sources and still have not raised enough money, you must begin approaching strangers, among them grantmakers.

If the unfamiliar prospective funder is a government agency, you can approach its staff directly. The best way to approach a foundation representative you don't know, however, is to go back to the list of foundation personnel that was reviewed by your volunteers, as described in Chapter Two. If the list shows that one of your volunteers knows someone at the foundation, ask the volunteer to contact that person. If you are approaching a staffed foundation and your volunteer knows one of the foundation trustees, the volunteer can ask the trustee to alert foundation staff that you will be calling to set up an appointment. If the foundation in question has no staff, your volunteer can ask if the two of you can meet with the trustee herself, or with another trustee, to discuss the project.

The main principle to keep in mind when making these arrangements is to identify the most powerful person associated with the grantmaker and get word to that person that you wish to explore the possibility of securing support. You may or may not meet with this individual directly. But if she is positively inclined toward whoever does make initial contact, the inclination will probably be conveyed to the foundation staff or her fellow trustees, and you will be assured of a receptive hearing. If someone in a leadership position introduces you, the staff will be as helpful as possible. Of course, if none of your volunteers knows an organizational leader, which is most often the case, you will have to approach a foundation program officer or agency staffer directly.

Opening the door at a new funding source requires that you think about many of the same issues you reflect on when selecting prospects from among your "friends and family." How does the activity for which you seek funding mesh with the grantmaker's priorities? Do the funder's previous grants demonstrate the same values that prompted your organization to develop this particular activity?

Let's say, for example, that you are seeking support for a project to prevent chemical dependency among teens. Is there any indication that the funder you are approaching cares about young people? About chemical dependency? About prevention methods? Do your homework by reviewing the funder's previous grants; this prepares you to respond when asked *why* you've come to a particular funder with a particular idea. Beyond this, other considerations depend, once again, on the situation.

Situation One: Development of a New Program, Service, or Organization. When you are seeking support for a new program or service, be sure to think through staffing and workload issues. If you are planning to use existing staff, be prepared to discuss which current responsibilities will be shifted to enable staff members to take on new responsibilities. The best spokesperson for the concept is usually the program's founder, since that person is usually the most passionate advocate. In fundraising as in romance, however, passion may be necessary but it is not sufficient. If your founder is not strong on logical, detailed discourse or compelling sales skills, then involve individuals who are, and develop a team approach.

Some funders are reluctant to help launch a new organization, as there are already more than half a million nonprofits competing with each other for philanthropic dollars. Given the fierce competition, you should be prepared to answer the question, is a new organization *really* necessary?

Situation Two: Meeting an Emergency Need. When you ask a prospective funder to help meet an emergency need or complete a stalled project, the main strategic issue is how you intend to avoid a recurrence of the crisis. You need to provide assurance that you won't get into the same bind in the future.

Situation Three: Meeting an Ongoing Need. When you approach a funder about providing support for ongoing needs, consider how providing such support might affect the funder. Unless the foundation's assets or income are growing significantly, supporting the same organization year after year will reduce the funds available for other purposes.

If you approach a staffed foundation, remember that its trustees are paying staff people to tell them how to achieve the optimum use of their philanthropic funds. It is highly unusual for a staffed foundation to provide ongoing support to the same organization year after year. On the other hand, if you approach a family foundation or a small foundation run by its trustees, ongoing support might be just the ticket to help busy trustees discharge their philanthropic responsibility without investing too much time.

Scenario B: Grantmaker Seeking Projects

The dynamic here is that of a feeding frenzy, with new money causing grantseekers to circle like sharks around a wounded mackerel. When funders are inundated by grantseekers and competition is intense, the clout of the person who makes the approach may matter less than familiarity—whether the person is known to the one being approached.

In such a frenzy, so many people seek a share that it may be difficult to get early and reliable information about the funder's priorities. Reading all the published information and attending all the public workshops or meetings is necessary, but not sufficient; information provided at public meetings or over a hotline is accessible to *all* grantseekers. This information cannot give you the competitive advantage needed to develop a successful strategy and win an award.

To get what you need, speak directly to a representative of the grantmaking organization. The closer the representative to the decision-making process, the more accurate and comprehensive the information she will have. But depending on the funding source, it may be unethical or illegal for the representative to provide information that gives a single grantseeker a competitive advantage; if your grantmaker seems at all reluctant to share information with you, be sensitive to this possibility.

When you approach a grantmaker that has issued a request for proposals or a broad agency announcement, try to discern what the funder wants to get out of making the awards. Think about the assets that you can bring to a joint venture, and what your organization has to offer as a partner. What relevant experience does your organization have? Whose skills could you draw on? What projects are you already conducting in related areas?

Marshaling Your Facts and Planning Your Approach

Scenario A: Organization Seeking Support

Before you contact a prospective funder, develop and assemble the facts that you should have available for your conversation. Consider preparing a written fact sheet before making first contact. Some information will need to be at your fingertips regardless of the type of support you are seeking; the rest is relevant only to specific situations.

Information Required for All Situations. First, think about the most effective way to introduce yourself. If you have an academic title, for example, it may or may not do some good to use it; some grantmakers may be impressed by a doctorate, but if you are dealing with people in a distinguished university, virtually everybody will have one and using yours may appear gauche.

If you are a member of a religious community, it is usually desirable to introduce yourself as "sister" or "father." People often adjust their language to reflect their respect of those who have chosen a religious life, and they may feel embarrassed if they learn of your commitment only *after* speaking with you.

If you are married and the person you call on knows your spouse but not you, it may help you to gain credibility by association if you mention your spouse when you introduce yourself.

Consider also whether to mention your position at the organization you represent. If you are the president or executive director, let the grantmaker know, as it means you have both programmatic and fiscal authority. If you are a member of the board of trustees, mention it; it means you have governing authority and are volunteering your time. If you also hold a professional position that carries some clout, as many volunteers do, it may be helpful to let the grantmaker know what that position is as well.

Second, don't forget that you are most likely immersed in what you do, and your perspective may be somewhat skewed. Remember that the person you're calling may have never heard of your organization, or may know very little about it. Often it helps to step back and recall your own first contact with the organization.

Can you remember your very first thought upon hearing the name of the organization? Reflect on those aspects of the organization's work that are most important to you and your colleagues, and then develop a two-or three-sentence description of what your organization does and how you became involved in the present enterprise. A review of your mission statement will help you relate today's undertaking to your organization's overall purpose. Your description should indicate why it makes sense for your organization to be involved in the grantmaker's new venture.

Third, point out your past successes as an indication that your future efforts are also likely to succeed. Assume that the grantmaker is unaware of your organization's accomplishments, and develop a one- or two-sentence summary that is impressive and memorable. Because grants are awarded to organizations rather than individuals, your summary should emphasize the organization's accomplishments, not your own. However, if your organization is new, you may need to point to the past accomplishments of individual staff members.

Fourth, because grantmakers deal with organizations and projects that represent a broad spectrum of size, scope, and impact, you need to indicate your location on the continuum. Let the grantmaker know as soon as possible what level of support you are seeking, and demonstrate that you have a fairly accurate sense of the scope of the project you are planning. This will be reflected in your budget. The scope of the project may change depending on the availability of funding, so you need to be flexible. But it's important to convey the impression that you're starting out with a clear idea of what you want to accomplish.

Information and Approaches for Situation One: Development of a New Program, Service, or Organization. As already emphasized, it is essential to show how supporting your activity will help advance the grantmaker's own agenda. For example, say you want to start a literacy program for adults, and the mission of the grantmaker you are approaching is to address problems of poverty. You should be prepared to show how your program will enable the participants to improve their economic standing by getting jobs if they're unemployed or better jobs if they're already employed. If the grantmaker is interested in education, stress that reading skills are essential to educational advancement and that participants in your program will have a higher rate of GED completion. Relate your project to the core values of the grantmaker.

As some funders are reluctant to get involved in launching new organizations, it's especially important to marshal certain facts:

- How many people need the service?
- What alternative approaches have been tried and found inadequate? Why didn't they work?

- What are the potential benefits of offering the new service?
- What will the social or economic costs be if the need is not addressed?

Answering these questions can demonstrate the need for a new program, service, or organization. But in addition, you should think through the major planning issues:

- Who will provide the service?
- Where will the service be provided?
- How will the service be priced?
- How will clients be recruited?

You may not be asked to provide detailed answers to such questions at this early stage, but you need to show that you are aware of these issues and plan to address them before you go much further.

Information and Approaches for Situation Two: Meeting an Emergency Need. As discussed earlier, such cases require that you present a strategy for avoiding the same kind of emergency in the future. Those who raise money for emergency needs often find themselves in awkward positions, as they may have had nothing to do with causing the emergency. Perhaps the manager who caused the emergency has been dismissed and you are the replacement: be careful about assigning blame. You never know who your predecessor's fans may be.

One strategy that works well if handled with care and sensitivity is to emphasize the risk involved in failing to respond to the emergency. You want to convey the importance and urgency of the situation without implying any obligation on the part of the grantmaker. You can strengthen your position by quantifying the possible outcomes.

Let's say, for example, that your predecessor allowed a swimming pool to fall into such disrepair that leaks now threaten the building that houses it. "If emergency repairs are not completed within 90 days," you might tell a potential donor, "we estimate that each month, 200 arthritis sufferers would be deprived of their aquatic therapy sessions, 500 children would be unable to take swimming lessons, and 300 adults would miss their daily swimming exercise. Besides the discomfort and inconvenience this would cause, our community's health care costs would increase, and our children's safety would be jeopardized. Also, the structural integrity of our $2.1 million building would be at risk, which would place our entire organization in serious fiscal jeopardy."

Information and Approaches for Situation Three: Meeting an Ongoing Need. To you it may seem obvious that your organization needs ongoing philanthropic support, but have an explanation ready for grantmakers anyway. For example, if you are involved in presenting concerts, you can make a compelling case that ticket revenues will never offset the cost of a performance, perhaps by calculating the vast increases in ticket prices that would be necessary if audience members had to pay a *pro rata* share of concert expenses.

Scenario B: Grantmaker Seeking Projects

Before you are swept away by the excitement of going after new money, stop to think about how a new project would fit into your organizational mission and priorities. If implementing it would take you away from what you really are about, don't succumb to the temptation. Make sure the opportunity is right for you before you invest time, energy, and money pursuing it. If you decide the project *does* make sense for your organization and that implementing it would fulfill some of your own agenda, you are ready to take the next step: preparing yourself to speak with the grantmaker. Do this by reflecting on the relevant resources you can bring to the table:

- To what constituencies do you have access?
- What kind of experience can you bring to bear on the problem the grantmaker wishes to address?
- How well do you understand the complexities of the problem?

When you can answer these questions, you will be well prepared for your initial conversation with the grantmaker.

Beginning the Relationship: The Critical Issues

Doing everything suggested in this chapter and the last one may seem like a lot of work to prepare for a phone call. It is necessary because of the basic power imbalance in the grantseeking relationship. You, the grantseeker, and your prospective grantmaker are both in the process of developing a partnership, even if you have different goals or motivations. And like any other two people about to become involved in a relationship, you both have two questions in mind.

First, what might this person contribute to the partnership I am contemplating? The grantseeker has a distinct advantage over the grantmaker in answering this, because you know what the grantmaker brings to the party: money. The grantmaker, on the other hand, is pretty much in the dark about the average grantseeker at this point. The purpose of assembling all the information recommended so far is to help the grantmaker see exactly how you could advance *her* agenda and make *her* look good.

The second question is, will this person actually deliver? In answering this, both you and your potential funder are equally in the dark. Neither of you yet has any way of knowing whether the other will deliver what is desired. You don't know in advance if the grantmaker will award you a grant, and the grantmaker doesn't know if you can or will fulfill the commitments you make. But your preparations are intended to help you to persuade the grantmaker that you will *indeed* deliver.

In the early stages of any relationship, each party will make inferences about the other. Uncertainty on both sides, however, maintains tension, and when people are uncertain if their needs will be met, they find it harder to attend fully to what the other person is saying. All the preparations you have been advised to make have one aim: to enable you to say things that will reduce the tension, so that the grantmaker can *listen* to you and *hear* what you are saying.

Now that you are prepared for your first conversation, we will detail both the text and subtext of this crucial exchange between you and your prospective grantmaker.

CHAPTER FOUR

MAKING YOUR FIRST CONVERSATION COUNT

Successful guerrillas almost invariably attach extreme importance to training and preparation . . . the training consists not simply in studying guerrilla military tactics . . . but in the manipulation of the political and economic and social forces that bear upon the outcome.

CHARLES W. THAYER, *GUERRILLA*

Following the steps outlined in Chapters Two and Three allows you to select appropriate grantmakers and develop basic strategies for approaching them. These were general preparations; now you need to prepare specifically for your first encounter. As you know, first impressions are very powerful, and they set the tone for everything that follows. Remember, in the relationship model of grantseeking, you are not merely trying to get a grant but to lay the groundwork for a partnership that can generate support for years to come. The first conversation, then, will be a complex interaction. You will convey and decode subtle, implied messages, as well as explicit information.

If you are like most people, you may be somewhat anxious about this conversation, and anxiety can impede your performance. The best way to reduce anxiety is to prepare thoroughly. The better prepared you are, the better you will perform, and giving it your best shot is what this chapter is about. There are two possible scenarios for an initial conversation: the *cold call*, an exchange between people who have never spoken before and have no knowledge of one another, and the *warm call*, an exchange preceded by a third party who knows you both asking the grantmaker to talk with you. For the sake of this discussion, we will assume that you are making a cold call—the more difficult variety. To position yourself for success, plan the conversation with the following objectives in mind:

- *Convey an explicit message.* When seeking a grant (Scenario A), you need to let the grantmaker know what your organization wants or needs. When responding to a grant opportunity (Scenario B), let the grantmaker know what your organization has to offer.
- *Convey an implicit message.* Specifically, you want the grantmaker to infer that you are a person with whom she would like to establish a relationship. This impression can be created through the subtext of your conversation.
- *Elicit information about the grantmaker's situation.* If you listen carefully, you can often gain valuable information about the grantmaker's program, priorities, and timetable.
- *Set up your first meeting*, nailing down all the details.

Placing Your Call

Take into account that there will probably be one or more rounds of "telephone tag" before you and your prospective grantmaker connect. Be prepared to leave messages and to speak with the grantmaker at a later date.

If the grantmaker is not in when you call, you may speak first with the receptionist, then with the grantmaker's secretary or administrative assistant. Remember that each of these people can be helpful in developing your relationship with the grantmaker. Assistants process your paperwork, provide (or impede) access, and have an intimate knowledge of the grantmaking process. Receptionists often keep track of where program officers are and what they're doing. It is clearly in your best interest to be on good terms with people in these support positions. One successful grantseeker observes Secretary's Week by sending flowers to the assistants of all his grantmakers.

If the receptionist puts you into the grantmaker's voice mail system, the message you leave will create your first impression on the grantmaker. It should therefore be clear and brief, but include enough details to make it easy to return your call. Allow for the operation of Murphy's Law—by the time your call is returned you will probably have misplaced or filed the fact sheet you prepared to guide yourself through the conversation. Make up a miniature, fail-safe version of the fact sheet on one or more sticky notes and place them on any phone you might conceivably pick up when the call comes in.

Once you reach the grantmaker, remember that your main goal is to communicate effectively. Find out right away if you can have her undivided attention at this particular time, or if she would prefer to speak with you later. If her tone of voice indicates that she is rushed, or if background noise makes it difficult for her to hear, ask if you can reschedule the conversation. The grantmaker will appreciate your consideration, and you will ensure that your message is *heard*.

Conveying Explicit Messages

When you finally find a good time to speak and the grantmaker is on the line, use your fact sheet. Here are three examples of how successful grantseekers applied the principles outlined in Chapters Two and Three to introduce themselves effectively.

Example One

The president of a new organization calls a grantmaker he has never met to discuss an idea he has for a project.

Background and Planning

In 1991, two years after the Ohio Aerospace Institute (OAI) was founded, its newly appointed president, Michael J. Salkind, decided he wanted to secure funding for meetings of interdisciplinary groups of scientists from government, industry, and academia who work on specific problems in aerospace-related technology. The purpose of getting them together in focus groups would be to promote communication that could lead to collaborative research, advancing American research agendas, and attracting large federal grants and contracts. Salkind believed these groups could help carry out OAI's mission of facilitating "collaboration among universities, industry and government to enhance the economic competitiveness of Ohio and the United States through research, education and technology adaptation."

In considering potential sponsors, Salkind dissected the various elements of the project and the values it demonstrated. Conceptually, it would have been easiest to identify a grantmaker whose primary goal was to promote collaborative research, or collaboration in general. Unfortunately, there *was* no such funder. So, revisiting OAI's mission statement, he focused on enhancing Ohio's economic competitiveness and soon realized that he knew of only one organization whose mission was to enhance the economic competitiveness of Ohio: namely, the Ohio State Department of Development.

The department was encouraging and enthusiastic, but it had no funding available for such projects at the time and so suggested approaching The Cleveland Foundation, the local community foundation, to discuss the economic development potential of the project. Researching The Cleveland Foundation by reading its recent annual reports, Salkind confirmed that it was an appropriate funding source. Its mission was to "enhance the quality of life for all residents of Greater Cleveland" and to "address the community's needs and opportunities." He also learned that the foundation had identified economic development as a key community need and was actively making grants in that area.

Salkind realized how the ends he had in mind intersected with the ends of The Cleveland Foundation: the focus groups could be presented as enhancing the economic development of Cleveland, the home community of OAI.[1] So he made contact, and this conversation ensued (note that in this and the following examples the questioner's words have been truncated to the basic questions of the model in Chapter Three).

The Conversation

[Q: Who are you?]

A: This is Michael Salkind, president of Ohio Aerospace Institute.

[Q: What's your story?]

A: OAI is a state-funded consortium of government, industry, and academia, established two years ago to promote collaborative research and encourage economic development in our area. I'm new in town. I'd like to get acquainted with you, and perhaps run by you an idea for a project I have been thinking about.

[Q: What's your track record?]

A: Before I took this job in Cleveland, I headed up R&D [research and development] for the Air Force, and I found in my twelve years there that collaboration is definitely a body-contact sport. By bringing people together—in person and by various electronic means—we found that we initiated more than double the usual number of new projects each year. And we saw this each of the last five years I was with the agency.

[As Salkind's purpose is to get acquainted, he doesn't specify the scope of the project he has in mind. Instead, he makes an appointment to meet with the grantmaker.]

Example Two

The CEO of a planning agency calls a grantmaker at a newly established foundation to discuss a new idea.

Background and Planning

Many buildings owned by the Catholic Diocese of Cleveland became underutilized or vacant as the number of children in Catholic schools dwindled and the number of priests and nuns declined. At the same time, the number of elderly persons was growing dramatically, and residential facilities that offered assisted living or nursing care were inadequate to meet the growing demand.

The diocesan organization that deals with social service needs is the Federation for Catholic Community Services, an umbrella organization overseeing the activities of thirty-seven social service agencies in its eight-county area of responsibility. At the recommendation of its strategic planning committee, the federation decided to look into converting some of the vacant or underutilized buildings into housing for elderly persons. Rev. Walter H. Jenne, then executive director of the federation, was assigned the task of raising the money needed to convert the first of these buildings, which would serve as a model for creating further such cost-effective facilities. Rev. Jenne knew that Joseph Bruening, a deeply religious Catholic who had recently died, had been committed to helping elderly people in Greater Cleveland. Bruening had left his fortune to establish a private foundation, and part of its mission was to carry on the founder's work on behalf of elderly people. So Rev. Jenne called the newly appointed executive secretary of the Bruening Foundation.

The Conversation

[Q: Who are you?]

A: This is Father Walt Jenne. I'm the executive director of the Federation for Catholic Community Services.

[Q: What's your story?]

A: Mr. Bruening was on our board, and I remember his commitment to helping his elderly neighbors. I wanted to let you know that we are thinking about an initiative along the lines that would have been of great interest to Joe. For the past six months, we've been involved in a strategic planning process, looking at community needs. It has highlighted our concern about the inadequacy of appropriate, affordable housing for elderly people, who are the fastest-growing segment of our population. Seven of our agencies provide services to elderly people, and they all report a growing but unmet need for assisted living and nursing care. We have extensive holdings of buildings and land, and would like to explore the possibility of using some of these resources to meet this need.

[Q: What's your track record?]

A: As you may be aware, Jennings Hall, our residential facility for elderly persons, has won several national and regional awards for innovative and responsive programming. We believe that by combining our expertise in program development with our existing facilities, we can make a major contribution to the community.

[Q: What is the scope of the project?]

A: We understand that there is HUD [the U.S. Department of Housing and Urban Development] and other government money for which we can apply, but we need to do a pilot project to establish our reputation in assisted living services, which is new for us. For $300,000 to $400,000, we believe we can rehab a vacant convent and convert it into assisted living units.

Example Three

The executive director of a social service organization calls a grantmaker to discuss the possibility of responding to an RFP [request for proposals] issued by a national foundation.

Background and Planning

Alice Kethley is executive director of the Benjamin Rose Institute (BRI), an organization that provides residential care and outreach services for elderly people and conducts gerontological research. She serves on several national committees and task forces concerned with various aspects of aging. When the Robert Wood Johnson Foundation issued an RFP related to new concepts in outreach, Kethley thought of a BRI project that might qualify.

The Conversation

[Q: Who are you?]

A: This is Alice Kethley in Cleveland. I believe we met at the President's Task Force on Aging in Washington last spring. I just received a copy of your "Partners in Caregiving" RFP, and I'm thinking about responding to it.

[Q: What's your story?]

A: My agency, the Benjamin Rose Institute, has just begun a planning process to develop a financially self-sufficient day care program for people with dementia. We have some ideas that will enable us to provide these much-needed services in a way that will help people with dementia stay independent longer.

[Q: What's your track record?]

A: Since 1928, BRI has been offering residential and community-based services for the elderly and conducting pioneering research in gerontology. For the last five years, our research department has been working with Dr. Peter Whitehouse, director of the Alzheimer's Center at University Hospitals of Cleveland. It's one of the four Centers of Excellence funded by the National Institutes on Aging.

We are developing programs that will use behavioral strategies to retard the progress of Alzheimer's disease.

[Q: What is the scope of the project?]

A: We believe that an investment of $400,000 to $500,000 will enable us to get our program off the ground, and to serve as many as ninety individuals within twelve months. We've run the numbers, and we believe we'll break even within eighteen months.

Conveying Implicit Messages

In addition to conveying *explicit* information during your first phone call with a grantmaker, you will need to communicate certain *implicit* messages as well. Here are the most important ones.

I understand the system.

Though grantmakers are accustomed to dealing with grantseeking novices, obviously it's tedious for them to explain over and over again how their grant-making processes work. If you show that you understand the basic steps involved in making grants, your dialogue will rise to a higher plane more quickly, and you will be able to engage in conversations about your work, the project you wish to undertake, or other topics of far greater interest to your grantmaker. Meaning-ful dialogue is at the heart and soul of good relationships, so you should try to get to it as soon as possible. The experience and knowledge you have gained through other relationships can be applied to a new one; for instance, in initial encounters, both parties decide whether they wish to establish a relationship. You certainly want to, and you can probably get that implicit message across fairly readily. Mak-ing the grantmaker want to have a relationship with you, however, is another mat-ter; it requires relaying another quite critical implicit message.

I am a credible person,
worthy of a relationship with you.

You want to make yourself appear attractive enough to interest the other person in getting to know you. The most basic requirement in any business relationship is trust, which is based on credibility; so you want to imply in every possible way that you are who you say you are, and that you will do what you say.

It takes time to convince a person that you are honest and trustworthy. Ulti-mately your credibility depends on your ability to deliver as promised, but a few simple strategies can help jump-start a grantmaker's initial impression of you as a credible person.

We talked earlier about using academic or religious titles when you introduce yourself. If used appropriately they can certainly add to your credibility; earning a terminal degree, for example, does not guarantee that you are honest or trustworthy but it does say something about your perseverance. If you are an officer in the military, you did what it took to achieve this distinction, and you should let your grantmaker know that you made a substantial contribution to your country's well-being. If you are a nun or a priest, you have made a commitment to the spiritual life, and your title can encourage the grantmaker to see you as a credible person and to take you seriously. At the very least, a title can set you apart from other grantseekers. That is highly desirable, as the average program officer must deal with a large number of applicants.

Another way to promote your credibility is to refer to a distinguished pedigree, if you have one. You might say, for example, "I began working on this problem when I was a graduate student at MIT" or "This project relates to the work I did to prepare for a congressional hearing."

You can also share with grantmakers your background of successful experience. For example, you might say something like this: "In my last position, I was responsible for turning around an organization with a large operating deficit and a high staff turnover rate. Within three years, we eliminated the accumulated deficit by tripling annual giving, and we reduced staff turnover to less than 5 percent. I believe that similar improvements are possible in my current situation."

I want to understand you better.

Next to credibility, the quality that most promotes sound relationship-building is a genuine interest in the other person. Show that you are interested in the grantmaker and her priorities. You might express yourself along these lines: "I'd be especially interested in learning more about the most effective economic development programs you are funding. I'd also like to know more about your foundation's priorities in terms of job creation and retention, and your view of the foundation's role in helping high-tech industry grow."

Some grantmakers are very forthcoming about their current interests and challenges, and that makes it easy for grantseekers to learn about the organization. Others may be less enthusiastic about sharing inside information. If this is the case, you can still imply your interest by indicating that you have done research on their past grantmaking activities. You can then begin building these relationships later, when they become comfortable enough to be more open with you.

In any case, your purpose is to determine whether your two organizations share core values that make it possible for you to work together. If these values drive you toward common goals, there is a rich potential for fruitful collaboration. To find out whether this potential exists, you will need to clearly articulate the ends your organization is pursuing, and how today's specific project provides a means to those ends. You will also need to ascertain what ends the grantmaker is seeking, and think about how your project may provide a means to achieving those as well.

Fruitful relationships between grantseekers and grantmakers develop when the interests of both coincide. Once the relationship is established, you can concentrate on weaving its fabric through hundreds of interactions over many years.

Setting Up a Meeting

If your telephone conversation has uncovered enough common ground, the grantmaker may suggest a meeting. If not, ask for one yourself.

No matter how well you have prepared for your conversation, and no matter how persuasive you have been, some grantmakers insist on seeing something in writing before they will agree to meet. This can present a major hurdle in developing a relationship, but when you encounter this demand you must comply. In the next chapter, we will discuss the best way to respond.

For now, let's assume that a meeting is in order. In making the arrangements, keep in mind that the grantmaker is the customer; though you should have a plan for how to proceed, remain flexible enough to accommodate your customer's preferences. Basically, however, planning the meeting requires asking the same questions as any good journalist: who, when, and where. Also ask how long the meeting will be and what will be on the agenda. Let's address each of these in order.

Who? As will be detailed in Chapter Six, your first meeting should include the president or CEO of your organization, a representative of your board, and a fund development staff person. For reasons of strategy as well as courtesy, it is important to let the grantmaker know in advance who will be representing your organization. For example, though you may be meeting with someone at the staff level, your board representative may know someone higher up in the grantmaker's organization; if you mention this to the staff person, she may invite the higher executive or trustee to stop by and say hello. Mentioning the participation of an important person raises your stock, so to speak, by showing the grantmaker that you can secure the involvement of powerful people.

When? Because the grantmaker is the customer, the meeting will be scheduled at *her* convenience. But as at least three people will be representing your organiza-

tion, you will need to do some advance planning before you make your call to identify a date that will work for everyone. Check the calendars of all those who will
represent your organization, and select at least three dates when they are all available. At least one of these will usually work for the grantmaker as well.

Where? Hold the meeting where it is convenient for the grantmaker—her office
unless she specifies otherwise. If you are planning to meet with a grantmaker
whose offices are out of town, schedule the meeting just as you would if the grantmaker were based in your own community.

   People who are new to grantseeking sometimes feel uneasy about admitting
that they're planning a trip for the sole purpose of meeting with a grantmaker, but
it is best to be honest. As a program officer from the Kellogg Foundation pointed
out at a recent meeting of grantmakers and grantseekers, "No one just 'happens
to be passing through' Battle Creek, Michigan." If you aren't completely honest
as you begin your relationship, you will jeopardize your credibility and undermine
the basis of a sound relationship.

How Long? It is important to know in advance how much time you will have with
the grantmaker. Strategically, the script you prepare for your meeting must fit the
time available. In terms of courtesy, it is important not to overstay the time allotted
for your visit unless the grantmaker suggests it. If the conversation is progressing
well, and she becomes so engaged that she wants to prolong the visit, your schedule should be flexible enough to accommodate this.

   When planning a series of meetings with grantmakers in another city, it is
probably impractical to plan more than four or five meetings in a day. First, there
are the logistic challenges of getting from one place to another in a timely fashion. Second, if you have already made the same "pitch" three times, it may be difficult to remember if you have mentioned a critical point in *this* meeting yet—or
in the meeting you just left.

What's the Agenda? As detailed in Chapter Six, there are two kinds of initial
meetings between grantseekers and grantmakers: the get-acquainted meeting and
the get-down-to-business meeting. In your telephone conversation, you will need
to determine which kind of meeting this one will be.

The Get-Acquainted Meeting. Ideally, you will have an opportunity to get acquainted
with your prospective grantmaker, using the initial meeting to learn more about
the individual, the interests of the organization, the immediate challenges it is facing, and any upcoming opportunities for grants that have not been publicized yet.
This information will enable you to identify activities that your grantmaker is most
likely to support. At the same time, you will be able to share your own interests

and areas of expertise, giving the grantmaker some sense of the ways in which you might become helpful to her.

Like a blind date, the get-acquainted meeting provides an opportunity to find out if you have mutual interests and wish to pursue a relationship.

The Get-Down-to-Business Meeting. This type of meeting focuses on the project you are seeking to fund. As it is also your first meeting with the grantmaker, you still need to provide some background on your organization. In essence, you will combine everything you would present in a get-acquainted meeting with a discussion of a specific project.

Even for a get-acquainted meeting, you should have one or two projects in mind and be ready to describe them; you never know when a get-acquainted meeting will suddenly turn into a get-down-to-business meeting. On hearing of a grant opportunity, for example, you may think of a project you are planning or already conducting that fits in, and it may be entirely appropriate to begin a dialogue about submitting a proposal.

Getting the Hang of It

Your first conversation with a grantmaker requires a greater investment of time and energy than subsequent encounters will. Grantseeking is like any other complex skill. Do you remember the first time you sat behind the wheel of a car, and how you felt as you listened to your driving instructor? At sixteen, you needed to think about every decision involved in driving: How far back do I need to brake to come to a full stop at the stop sign? Where's that little stick that makes the turn signal come on? But with experience, driving becomes automatic, and the same is true of grantseeking. Niccolò Machiavelli, the master strategist, may have said it best when he observed that "he who does not lay his foundations beforehand may by great abilities do so afterwards, although with great trouble to the architect and danger to the building."[2]

You are the architect of the grantseeker-grantmaker relationship. If you take care in laying the foundations, the structure will be sound and it will endure.

The essential elements of guerrilla tactics must always be kept in mind. These are: perfect knowledge of the ground; surveillance and foresight . . . vigilance over all the secondary roads that can bring support . . . intimacy with people in the zone so as to have sure help from them . . . total mobility; and the possibility of counting on reserves.

CHE GUEVARA, *GUERRILLA WARFARE*

CHAPTER FIVE

"SEND ME SOMETHING IN WRITING": DOCUMENTS THAT GET RESULTS

A small notebook and pen or pencil for taking notes and for letters to the outside or communication with other guerrilla bands ought always to be a part of the guerrilla fighter's equipment.

CHE GUEVARA, *GUERRILLA WARFARE*

When a grantmaker insists on seeing something in writing before agreeing to meet with you, what you have is a classic case of conflicting goals. You're ready to start talking, to establish your relationship. She wants a quick way to screen serious, worthwhile grantseekers from those who may waste her time. Fortunately, you can turn this lemon into lemonade by adopting a different perspective.

Consider the grantmaker's position. In the early stages of the relationship, grantmakers may have all the control and power, but their situations are far from easy; they are inundated by requests for appointments from grantseekers and by proposals that must be reviewed. As noted in Chapter One, there are only a few thousand professionals working full-time for U.S. foundations but more than half a million nonprofit organizations competing for their attention and that of the busy individuals who volunteer in foundation work. Grantmaking professionals in the public sector are also swamped with requests for more meetings than there are hours in the day, and for several times more dollars than are available. All these people need some way to separate those who merit their attention from those who don't.

The dynamic in this situation is similar to that of a job seeker and a prospective employer in any field where job seekers are more plentiful than jobs. Just as employers will ask to see a résumé or *curriculum vitae* before interviewing a candidate, so many grantmakers will ask to see a preliminary document before meeting with you. And just as preparing a résumé can help clarify the significance of your past experience and articulate goals for your next position, preparing a preliminary document for a grantmaker can be an opportunity to consolidate your thinking and clarify key issues.

Planning Your Response

Keep in mind that this preliminary document, like a résumé or indeed any business document, may be necessary but it is not sufficient. Yes, you will need to prepare the document carefully. You will need to be cogent and persuasive. You will need to follow the prescribed format and content, present your document in a professional way, and submit it in a timely fashion. But all this will not be sufficient to secure a grant. A document is only part of the story—one element in a complex series of transactions in making a deal.

That said, the first order of business is to respond promptly to the grantmaker's request and to submit a document of high quality. Your goal should be to prepare as brief and cogent a document as possible.

Three Types of Documents

The first decision to be made is what kind of document you will provide. There are three basic types: the *letter*, the *concept paper*, and the *white paper* or position paper. Most often, the grantmaker will specify which one she wants, and you will comply. If she leaves it open, you can choose whichever serves you best.

Although a prompt submission is advantageous, you shouldn't let yourself be pressured into preparing your document too hastily. Time invested in planning and thinking through strategic issues will pay significant dividends in the quality of the relationship developed.

Key Elements of the Document

Whether or not you have the option of deciding which kind of document to prepare, these are the key elements to consider:

- Purpose; the desired outcome
- Role of the document in building the relationship between you and the grantmaker
- Structure
- Strategic content
- Voice or tone

The Letter

If the grantmaker doesn't specify which kind of document she wants, you should generally prepare a letter, as it is the least formal and the closest to a conversation. Remember, it is conversations and the building of relationships, not the submission of documents, that wins grants.

Purpose

The purpose of a letter, like that of an initial telephone conversation, is to establish or enhance your relationship with the grantmaker. You are seeking the same specific outcome: to persuade the grantmaker to meet with you. All other choices you make in developing the document should relate to this goal.

Role in the Relationship

You may have no choice but to comply with the grantmaker's request for a document, but you can still present yourself in it as a colleague rather than a prostrate supplicant. Concentrate on the challenges of developing the project and the long-term funding strategies—the "big picture." If you emphasize your need to secure immediate grant support, you come off as a supplicant and an undesirable partner.

You can also influence the grantmaker's perception of you by seeking her advice; approach her as a resource, not as an obstacle between you and the grant. Doing so often succeeds for two reasons.

First, even if you are very sophisticated and knowledgeable, your thinking and planning can probably benefit from grantmaker input; grantmakers are often astute, thoughtful, and insightful people. They have much more experience than most grantseekers in observing a wide variety of projects, and they often have a keen sense of what will work and what will not. Many grant-funded projects reflect a cutting-edge approach, or even an experimental one. Grantmakers tend to develop a sixth sense about which kinds of experiments hold promise and which do not. Their perspective helps them to identify weaknesses in planning and to offer ideas that can strengthen a project.

Second, a frequent stumbling block encountered by grantseekers is the question grantmakers inevitably pose: "How do you intend to support this project after the grant support expires?" You may not have a ready answer when the project is conceived, but if you address the issue of long-term funding early on, you give yourself more time to develop sound strategies, increasing your project's odds of long-term success. The advantage of considering grantmakers as resource people is that with their experience in observing how projects progress from drawing board to full functioning, they can share with you long-term funding strategies that have been successful for similar projects. If you are the one to initiate the discussion of long-term funding, you demonstrate seriousness, impress the grantmaker, and increase your chances of securing an immediate grant.

Structure

The letter should follow this logical progression: background of the organization, background of the project, description of the problem or statement of need, description of the project, budget narrative, request for meeting, and budget summary. As you can see, this outline is similar to the one you used to plan your initial telephone conversation; actually, it can serve as the framework for virtually all communications with grantmakers, including concept papers and grant proposals.

Strategic Content

Your letter should provide enough information to convince the grantmaker that you have a full command of the situation and knowledge of the field, without overloading her with details. Remember, the letter is not a proposal; if you make it too detailed, the grantmaker may even *consider* it a proposal and evaluate it accordingly. This could bring your dialogue to a premature close.

Strategically, the most important part of your letter is the indication that, now that you have complied with the request for written communication, you will be calling to set up a meeting. By stating that you will make the call, you acknowledge the grantmaker's superior power, at least at this stage of the relationship. A typical closing sentence might be: "I will call within two weeks to set up a convenient time for us to meet and discuss these ideas." Specify two or three weeks; that's enough time for the grantmaker to read your letter but not so much that she will have forgotten it when you call.

Voice

The voice or tone of your letter should be businesslike, but warmer and more personal than a proposal or concept paper. Make it seem like a conversation, rather than a summary of your annual report:

Formal Document	*Informal Expression in Letter*
Background of the organization	"Here's who we are."
Background of the project	"Here's our situation."
Description of the problem	"Here's the problem (need) we've identified."
Description of the project	"Here's an idea we have to solve the problem [meet the need]."

The Concept Paper

A concept paper is a document that describes an idea you have for a project. If your grantmaker requests a concept paper, or you decide that preparing such a document is the most appropriate course of action, keep the following points in mind.

Purpose

A concept paper is intended to capture the interest and imagination of the grantmaker. Although a grant is never made on the basis of a concept paper alone, the document can certainly generate a desire to support your project; use it to convince the grantmaker to meet with you to explore in greater detail the potential of your idea.

Role in the Relationship

Because the purpose of a concept paper is to share an idea, submitting one implies a high level of trust, which is the cornerstone of a good working relationship. It demonstrates your confidence that the grantmaker will respect your ownership of the idea whether or not she supports it financially, and that she will not share it inappropriately with others. As the advertisement reproduced in Figure 5.1 demonstrates, ideas are not only the most valuable commodity in our culture, but the most fragile.

By sharing your concepts with grantmakers, you get them involved at a very early stage—and in the grantseeking enterprise, the sooner they are involved, the better.

Structure

The structure of the concept paper is similar to that of the letter. If you have already established a relationship with a grantmaker who knows something about your organization, you can cover the background very briefly and then move on to a discussion of the situation that prompted you to develop your idea.

Strategic Content

The concept paper is similar to an essay in which you run an idea up the flagpole to see who salutes; it is the most cerebral of preliminary documents. In it, emphasize why, rather than how, a project should be undertaken. Draw attention to

FIGURE 5.1. AN IDEA IS A FRAGILE THING.

It was just an idea.

An idea is a fragile thing. Turning it off is much easier than keeping it lit.

A company called TRW lives on ideas. So we look for people who have them and for people who won't snuff them out. In recent years TRW has been issued hundreds of patents in such diverse fields as fiber optics, space, lasers and transportation electronics.

Those ideas shone because somebody had them and somebody helped them. And nobody turned them off.

Tomorrow is taking shape at a company called TRW.

the creative and innovative aspects of your approach and how it differs from others tried in the past.

Voice

When novice grantseekers prepare documents, they often adopt a formal style whether it is called for or not. They use highly technical terms and language that is stilted and impersonal; their writing is characterized by a high level of abstraction and a preponderance of the passive voice. Such documents tend to sound as though they are written *by* one organization *for* another, rather than by one person for another person. But things don't get done by organizations, only by people. Shy individuals like to hide behind the protective mask of an organization; unfortunately, this creates distance between grantseeker and grantmaker, and distance rarely enhances a relationship.

Author William Mengerink suggests that grantseekers prepare all their documents as if they were writing a letter to Aunt Sylvia, a family member of whom they are fond.[1] It's a good idea. Your grantmaker may not be quite as receptive as a relative who loves you, but will probably prefer to hear from a real person instead of an impersonal organization or office. Take the risk of being visible and identifiable as the person responsible for the conception of a project or the shaping of a plan or event. And whenever possible, make your concept more concrete by including vignettes about real people; these examples make it easier for the grantmaker to remember your project.

The White Paper

If your grantmaker requests a white paper (position paper), or you learn of an opportunity to submit one, then rejoice: your chances of success are excellent, because the process has been initiated by the grantmaker. As discussed in Chapter One, grant programs begin when a grantmaker decides to address a problem by investing money in it. Sometimes grantmakers realize that people in the field may have more expertise or knowledge of current developments than they do, and so decide to shape more meaningful programs by soliciting input from practitioners or researchers. When this occurs, one of two things may happen.

Grantmakers on a short timetable may go to their Rolodexes and call a few people, usually current or former grantees, and talk with them. If you are one of these people, you may not need this book, but few grantseekers achieve this stature. Beyond this casual networking approach, a grantmaker may request white papers. What makes this situation so promising for grantseekers? First, the grantmaker is taking the initiative; and second, communication is beginning at an early stage. In other situations, grantseekers are supplicants and all power is held by the grantmakers. But when grantseekers are solicited for white papers, they are being approached as colleagues who have information that the grantmakers need. In our society information is the most valuable currency, and when a grantmaker acknowledges that you, the grantseeker, possess this resource, it shifts the balance of power in the relationship.

Also, when the grant program is still being formulated you work with the grantmaker at the earliest possible stage. You can benefit in many ways from this early involvement. Just as a parent can shape a child's values and development, people involved in the formative stages of a project can influence how it develops; furthermore, early involvement provides more time for you and your grantmaker to become familiar and comfortable with one another. In grantmaking as in other enterprises, people are apt to do business with people they know rather than with strangers. So your early involvement will give you an advantage over competitors who enter the process at a later stage.

Purpose

Your goal should be to impress grantmakers by making them understand that you are a member of the new aristocracy of our information society—an "information overlord." You want to show that your knowledge is both broad and deep, that your information is up-to-the-minute, and that your contacts include leaders in your field. If you succeed, you will achieve the desired outcome: the grantmaker will seek to continue the dialogue and eventually request a formal proposal.

Role in the Relationship

The preparation of a white paper presents a great opportunity to establish yourself in the eyes of the grantmaker as a most attractive potential business partner by demonstrating that you are both well informed and well connected. The white paper should also imply that you can make the grantmaker look good; if you can provide useful information and help her stand out among her peers and colleagues, you will earn a high degree of respect and gratitude.

This also puts you in good standing for subsequent interactions, including the preparation and submission of a proposal. In any relationship, you may be called upon to play several roles, but the first one usually makes the strongest impression; your initial role as a colleague and helper will influence a grantmaker's perception of you when you become a competitive grantseeker. Your proposal, of course, will be reviewed along with all the others, but many of these will be viewed as coming from supplicants.

Structure

Your white paper should include the following elements in the following order:

- Description of the issue or problem—its scope, size, shape, and dynamics
- Impact of the issue or problem
- Previous attempt(s) to address the issue or solve the problem
- Description of your new solution and why it holds greater promise than previous efforts
- Potential benefits of implementing your new solution

Strategic Content

Each of the above elements should be approached with your purpose clearly in mind. Because the grantmaker who solicits a white paper usually has a working knowledge of the issue or problem, your description of it can usually be covered briefly, but if you are not sure how much detail the grantmaker wants, you have a wonderful opportunity to open the dialogue by asking about it directly. In the course of your conversation, you can gain a lot of useful information about the program and the grantmaker's interests.

Take care in preparing the section on previous attempts to solve the problem and the one on the solution you propose, because the people who suggested previous solutions may be known to the grantmaker; she may even have supported some of their earlier work. For that matter, some of them are almost certainly preparing white papers to compete with yours. So show proper respect for the work that preceded your own by treading lightly in discussing previous efforts that failed or experienced only limited success.

Concentrate on the section that describes the potential benefits of implementing your proposed solution. This section has the greatest potential to persuade the grantmaker to support your project. Keep focused on your ultimate purpose: you are trying to get a grant, not preparing an academic treatise.

Voice

Because the white paper calls for a fairly high level of abstraction, it is tempting to adopt an academic tone and to write from a stance that is distant and aloof. But to make your submission memorable, include as many concrete examples and statistics as possible. These demonstrate your grasp of details and perhaps even of arcane data, which is bound to impress your grantmaker.

Before You Start to Write

Whether you're generating a letter, concept paper, or white paper, before you sit down to draft it, think through your strategy. The first step is to define your purpose and to outline the result you hope to achieve. Think about what interests the grantmaker and try to match your presentation to those interests.

Outline all the information you have available, and identify any gaps to be filled in. Try to identify the best sources for the information you lack. If your initial outline raises questions, write them down and figure out how they can best be answered, and by whom. As you begin to draft your document, try to answer these questions:

- Who will direct the project?
- Who will benefit from it?
- What activities will need to be carried out?
- Who will carry them out?
- What human and physical resources, and in what quantity, will be needed to carry out these activities?
- Where will these resources come from?
- What will they cost?
- How will you know when you have succeeded?
- How will the world be different once you have succeeded?

Answering these questions even in summary form may require a considerable investment of time and energy, so you will get the job done faster if several people gather the information. Once all of it has been assembled, select one person to write your document. Just as a symphony orchestra sounds better with a conductor in charge, your document will read better and make a stronger impression if it is written in one voice.

After your first telephone conversation and after you've submitted something in writing, if asked to do so, you are ready to prepare for your first meeting with the grantmaker.

The guerrilla . . . turns the hazards of the terrain to his advantage and makes an ally of tropic rains, heavy snow, intense heat, and freezing cold.

CHE GUEVARA, *GUERRILLA WARFARE*

CHAPTER SIX

PLANNING FOR A SUCCESSFUL MEETING (BEFORE SUBMITTING YOUR PROPOSAL)

Every guerrilla leader in history has stressed the need for a highly organized, thoroughly disciplined core of dedicated fighters as a prerequisite for a successful guerrilla operation.

CHARLES W. THAYER, *GUERRILLA*

Telephone conversations work well for initial contacts and interim communications, and letters or other written documents are useful for conveying complex information and formal agreements. But meetings are the only way to advance a relationship significantly.

As discussed in Chapter Five, after making your initial telephone contact with the grantmaker, you may be invited to attend a get-acquainted meeting or a get-down-to-business meeting. In this chapter, we examine these in detail.

In grantseeking, the other kinds of meetings you frequently encounter are the postsubmission office visit and the site visit. Both normally take place after you have submitted your formal proposal. Following the process in chronological order, then, Chapter Seven describes the process of preparing your proposal, and Chapter Eight discusses these other two kinds of meetings. The first order of business, however, is to understand the principles that apply to conducting any successful meeting.

Principles of Successful Meetings

In the highly competitive arena of grantseeking, you will be vying with numerous other organizations for the attention of the grantmaker. As in virtually all other endeavors, it is a combination of preparation, flexibility, and agility that often separates the winners from the losers.

Although careful preparation is essential, so is the ability to improvise; you can never tell exactly how a meeting will progress or a conversation will evolve. You need to be able to think on your feet and respond appropriately to any exigencies or opportunities that arise. Preparing for meetings is a lot like preparing for a theatrical production: you need to devote considerable forethought to casting, scripting, costuming, staging, and rehearsals. But when the curtain goes up, you still need spontaneity to give a convincing performance and win over your audience.

Casting

The people you select to participate in your meeting should represent all the relevant constituencies, and each should be well informed and highly credible. If, for instance, your project is an educational program that involves introducing new courses of study, those who speak about it would ideally include the faculty members designing the courses. As you select participants, concentrate on how they function and perform rather than on their positions or titles. The purpose of the team is to make an impression, so make sure you have all the right elements to do it.

In building a team, quality is always more important than quantity. Consider all the following possible elements: staff leadership, program staff, lay leadership, fundraising staff, representatives of collaborating organizations, current or potential co-funders, and clients or consumers of your services.

Staff Leadership. If at all possible, involve your top administrator—the CEO, president, or executive director. If that cannot be done, select someone as high in the administration as possible; you want somebody who truly represents the organization as a whole so as to demonstrate institutional support for and interest in developing a relationship with the grantmaker.

Remember, it is crucial to think about how people function. If you're lucky, your CEO is also your resident visionary—the person who best articulates the organization's goals and direction. But if your CEO is primarily a manager and another staff member is the visionary, bring both to the meeting; both management skills and vision are essential.

Program Staff. Your project director—principal investigator in scientific projects—should play the most prominent role in the presentation; this person's work is what the grantmaker is being asked to support. However, a project director may be a creative genius, a wonderful technician, or a superb team manager without having great selling skills, and your purpose in this meeting is to make an effective sales presentation.

Whatever your project director's talents, your preparation should include a rehearsal of that person's presentation, with your resident sales expert on hand to critique it. In nonprofit organizations, your best critic is usually (but not always) someone who works in public relations or fund development. Some project directors may be skeptical or even resentful of such criticism. They believe that the sales aspects of a presentation are irrelevant to winning an award, cherishing the quaint notion that grants are awarded on the basis of merit alone, and assume that a distinguished track record speaks for itself. You must disabuse such project directors of their illusions. Today's grantseeking environment is very competitive, and your project director needs to understand that winning an award depends on selling the personnel, not just the quality of their work.

Volunteer Leadership. Whenever possible, involve the chairman or another member of your board, as that body is morally, legally, and financially responsible for the organization. When a volunteer leader donates time and energy, it demonstrates to the grantmaker that relationships with such individuals are important to your organization. It also emphasizes that your lay leadership is involved in the project and committed to supporting it. If no board member is available, try to involve another volunteer leader, preferably someone with clout in the community.

Fundraising Staff. Your development officer will eventually play a key role in communicating with the grantmaker, so it is wise to include her at the outset. It is the responsibility of development staff to cultivate, orchestrate, and maintain relationships with donors; for this reason, the development officer should identify the best candidates for participation in the meeting, prepare the script, and direct the rehearsals.

During the meeting, your development officer should provide information as needed, monitor progress, and keep things moving if the meeting should threaten to stall. She should observe any verbal and nonverbal cues the grantmaker may provide, and intervene if she picks up anything significant. Otherwise, the development officer should keep a low profile, as her role is secondary. She is in a perfect position to take notes, which allows the other participants to give their full attention to the conversation. After the meeting, the development officer can help analyze what transpired and provide input on what should be done next.

Representatives of Collaborating Organizations. If other organizations are collaborating with yours on the project, their representatives should participate in the meeting to demonstrate their involvement in planning and their commitment to implementation. They should be prepared to explain from *their* perspective how the collaboration came about and how the relationship is progressing.

Current or Potential Co-Funders. If other grantmakers are supporting your project, or giving it serious consideration, be sure to include them in the meeting. Their financial support is the strongest encouragement another prospective funder can receive. If it is not possible or practical for co-funders to join you in person, consider asking them to participate by telephone, either during or after the meeting.

Clients or Consumers of Your Services. Clients and other beneficiaries of an organization's services are often overlooked, but well worth considering. Everyone knows, as the adage says, that the proof is in the pudding, so when people who have actually used your services are willing to talk about their personal experiences, it can powerfully advance your case. Depending on the type of organization, your clients or consumers may include alumni, patients, parents, or other family members. Not every constituency needs to be represented at every meeting, but a diverse team can represent your organization in a comprehensive way. It can also demonstrate that your organization is serious about establishing a relationship with the grantmaker.

Scripting

As a grantseeker, your job consists largely of communication. What is said, who says it, and how it is said are all crucial to your success. If you are like most people, you probably feel anxious about talking to someone who has the power to award or withhold funds. But anxiety is as detrimental to the grantseeker as a pulled muscle is to the athlete, and just as the best way to avoid a muscle pull is to warm up properly, the best way to avoid meeting anxiety is to plan carefully.

You may be tempted to prepare a verbatim script, so that each participant says exactly the right thing. But this makes it almost impossible to maintain a sense of spontaneity and to project your personal style. A list of bulleted points will probably serve you better. As Mao Tse-tung wisely counseled, "While we should think through our plans at length, we should avoid overly subtle plans."[1]

The cardinal principles of preparing a script are these:

- Do not plan to say too much; leave time for listening. Plan to say everything you believe needs to be said in about half the time allocated for the meeting. That will leave the grantmaker time to respond and get involved in the process. Encourage your grantmaker to provide feedback, ask questions, and make suggestions.
- Plan to spend some time making small talk at the beginning of the meeting. Some novice grantseekers are so anxious that they leap right in to their spiel. This is usually not wise. A little introductory conversation allows you to identify mutual interests and bond with grantmakers by learning something about them

as people. Some disdain small talk as a waste of time, but it's like foreplay in sex: it's possible to do without it, but the benefits are usually well worth the time.

- Convey key points of your message in more than one medium. People process information in several different ways, and listening to words is only one of them. Some people remember graphics more vividly than words, and graphic presentations are especially helpful to visual learners. Charts, graphs, and tables impress people who process information visually.

This last point deserves more elaboration. New low-cost computer software packages make it easy to produce high-quality, professional-looking visual aids, but they have also raised people's expectations dramatically; be aware that an amateurish presentation implies that you lack professionalism in other areas. Avoid typewritten transparencies at all costs, and use handwritten transparencies only when you're taking "public notes" in a spontaneous dialogue.

Beyond briefing notes, charts, and graphs, you may want to consider producing a videotape. If you have a short video (no longer than ten minutes) that describes your project, it can be shown during your meeting or left for the grantmaker to review whenever convenient. But if you want to show a video during the meeting, be sure to confirm in advance that the grantmaker can accommodate it easily and is willing to use valuable meeting time for it.

Sometimes the best way to make a message memorable is to present physical objects, but be sensitive about it. On one occasion, the executive director of the Cleveland Eye Bank wanted to demonstrate to a grantmaker the need for more storage equipment. The most dramatic way to do this was to show the program officer an actual ocular storage device and explain that the current storage unit could hold only half as many chambers as needed to be stored. In this instance, we asked the program officer if was okay to show him an actual device, knowing that some people might be squeamish. On another occasion, we were presenting information about a project that would advance neurosurgery, and we had produced a video showing actual surgery. Before leaving the video with the grantmakers, we made sure to ask if they would be comfortable viewing it.

Finally, keep in mind that visual aids should serve a supporting role and never claim center stage. If you're feeling anxious, you may be tempted to spend more time fussing with your transparencies than looking the grantmaker in the eye. Try not to succumb to this temptation. Keep focused on your objectives: to communicate with your grantmaker and to establish or advance the relationship.

Costuming

Just as guerrilla soldiers always dress appropriately for the terrain, so should you. The dress code at most foundations and government agencies is fairly conservative.

You will usually fit in at a meeting with a grantmaker if you dress as you would for a job interview at a bank, brokerage house, or IBM.

If you're planning an all-day series of meetings, be sure to wear comfortable shoes; when your feet hurt, it can be difficult to concentrate on the conversation. As Che Guevara advised guerrillas, "Shoes should be of the best possible construction and also, since without good shoes marches are very difficult, they should be one of the first articles laid up in reserve."[2]

If your meeting involves a meal, be conservative in your choice of restaurant and selections from the menu. You want to create an impression of prudence and responsibility, so a nice but modestly priced restaurant is usually a better choice than a flashy, expensive one. Avoid high-priced menu items, and always forego alcohol. Save the big-ticket meals and the champagne for your celebration *after* you get the grant.

Staging

An intentional seating plan for your meeting can make your conversation and presentation more effective. Your chief spokesperson should be positioned so that she can easily make eye contact with and show graphic displays or objects to the grantmaker. If possible, your volunteer leader should sit next to your CEO to show that the board supports the staff. Ideally, your development officer should sit where she can signal discreetly to the other staff and to volunteer leaders. Rehearse the meeting, discussing your signal system and making sure everyone knows how to respond.

Rehearsals

The Worst-Case Scenario. Mock battles play an extremely valuable training role in the military; similarly, rehearsals can substantially improve your performance in a meeting. If you're feeling anxious, a dry run may reduce your anxiety.

In a rehearsal, your development officer should take the role of the grantmaker. The best way to prepare is to try to anticipate the most difficult questions the grantmaker could ask. For example:

- Why is your organization running a deficit, and what are you going to do about it?
- Why did the former CEO resign suddenly?
- What were the *real* issues behind the faculty strike?

In your preparation, get all the skeletons out of the closet and develop credible and honest answers to every question. If you need help, call in your public relations person. When everyone is satisfied that you have adequately addressed all the most challenging questions, relax; the actual meeting is never as difficult as the worst-case scenario.

Planned Spontaneity. In meetings with grantmakers, each participant has in mind what to say but may decide to change either the order or substance in response to what arises. Such flexibility keeps your presentation lively, natural, and spontaneous. One purpose of rehearsing is to make each participant more aware of time. Your team needs to develop a collective sense of how much detail can be presented without exceeding the time allotted for the meeting or cutting into the time required for the grantmaker to get involved.

Attitude, Attitude, Attitude. In real estate, it's often said that the three most important considerations are location, location, and location. In grantseeking or any other kind of selling, the three most important considerations are attitude, attitude, and attitude. Your team will perform better if you think about this in advance and talk about it during rehearsal.

In grantseeking, the most successful attitude is one of respectful receptiveness and responsiveness, which is best demonstrated by attending carefully to what the grantmaker has to say. Respect in any relationship is a complex matter; if you want to develop a viable, fruitful relationship, the respect must be sincere. As you get to know grantmakers, they will probably earn your respect, but you must assume that they deserve it from the beginning. Show that you are attentive and responsive by literally taking note of all your grantmaker's suggestions. If the suggestions are explicit, simply write them down and follow up on them. Often, however, they can only be inferred; because so much communication is subtle and so many important points may only be implied, all your attendees should be prepared to listen carefully and take responsibility for analyzing both what has been *said* and what has been *implied*. If the grantmaker poses a question and you do not have the answer at your fingertips, don't get in trouble by making one up; just make note of it, promise to get the answer, and respond in a timely fashion after the meeting. Be sure to keep a copy of your response for future reference.

You want to be as responsive as possible, but there is a fine line between being respectfully responsive and being overly deferential or obsequious. Grantmakers are all too aware of the superior power of their position. One grantmaker confessed that on the day she accepted a position as a program officer with the largest foundation in town, "I heard my last sincere compliment, lost my last real friend, and paid for my last lunch." This may be a slight exaggeration, but grantmakers do have strong negative feelings about grantseekers who fawn on them and curry favor; this behavior erodes the credibility upon which sound relationships are built.

As discussed in Chapter One, grantmakers are customers of grantseekers, but the most successful grantseekers know that there is more to the relationship. View your grantmaker as not merely a provider of financial support, but as a helpful colleague and resource person. This is an unusual and multifaceted relationship with few analogies outside the grantseeking arena. If you can think of your grant-maker as a colleague, you will improve your chances of building a relationship based on mutual respect. And that is essential to a sound, enduring partnership.

Conducting Successful Meetings

The Get-Acquainted Meeting

As indicated in Chapter Four, your purpose in a get-acquainted meeting is to influ-ence the grantmaker to continue the relationship. One of your strategic goals is to learn if there are upcoming grant opportunities for which you might qualify.

An ideal outcome is for the grantmaker to invite you to submit something in writing. Your document then will outline a concept that could be developed into a project, which the grantmaker might then consider supporting. Note how many steps come between the initial conversation and even the possibility of a grant; this is not a sport for the impatient!

In this meeting, you will introduce the grantmaker to your organization. The participants should thus include only those individuals who represent the whole organization: your CEO, a volunteer leader, and a fundraising professional.

Conducting the Meeting. After preliminary small talk, your participants should introduce themselves or be introduced by the CEO. These introductions should emphasize the roles they play in the organization, and it is also helpful to mention any prior experience or aspect of their backgrounds that make them credible rep-resentatives. Say, for example, "This is George Thomas, the president of Data-tronix. He's the chairman of our board and led our recent $5 million capital campaign. He's been on the board for six years." Or perhaps, "Let me intro-duce you to Cynthia Topping, our vice president for development. She did her undergraduate work at our college. She served as development director for the Girl Scouts for five years before coming back to us."

After each participant has been introduced, introduce your organization: sum-marize its mission, character, services, constituencies, and history. For example: "Our college has 4,000 students. We specialize in career-enhancing programs for employed adult learners. We got our start back in 1897 as the vocational training program affiliated with the YMCA, but we've been independent and fully accredited since 1978. We are ranked fourth among thirty schools in our category by *U.S. News and World Report.* We have the lowest tuition of any private school in our state, and of those students who matriculate, over 80 percent graduate."

Or the representative of a hospice program might say: "Ours was the first hospice in the state, and we've been serving this area since 1979. Today, we are the largest facility in the state, with an average daily census of over 400 patients and family members. Our mission is to provide comfort-oriented home care for terminally ill patients and their families. We offer a holistic approach to care for the dying. We promote the highest possible quality of life during the final months or days of life, and we strive to make the terminal phase and death itself painless."

Once you have introduced your organization, the conversation should turn to recent successful programs and ideas for new initiatives you are considering. For instance, the spokesperson for the college might explain: "The majority of our students are employed adults, attending school on a part-time basis at night. While this population is unusual for an institution of higher education today, our perspective enables us to look at issues that will become crucial to American higher education in the decades to come. More and more, higher education is serving adults who are seeking to advance their careers or to prepare for a midlife career change. The first issue we would like to discuss with you is how to accelerate 'time to degree' for students who are going to school to advance their careers. The second issue is how to make our curriculum more relevant to the new, collaborative models in the business world, as our economy moves from a manufacturing base to an information base."

The representative of the hospice might say: "Though we believe we are providing the best possible service to adults with families, we frequently get calls from people we really can't help in our current configuration. One group for whom we can provide only limited services is families with terminally ill children. As you can imagine, dying children need different kinds of services than adults. For instance, they need little legal help or relationship counseling, but they do need substantial help in understanding what is happening to them. And young siblings of dying children need support in many ways that are unique to their age group. One of the issues we would like to discuss with you is the needs of this population."

When you talk about key issues facing the organization, be sure that your volunteer leader makes a substantive contribution. This will assure the grantmaker that your board is involved in and aware of the strategic issues, and that your volunteer was not invited along merely as window dressing.

After you have outlined one or two key issues and asked for the benefit of the grantmaker's thinking, the meeting should be turned over to the grantmaker for a response. At this point, the grantmaker may well volunteer that a new grant opportunity is being planned, and that you might want to develop a project dealing with the issue you have raised. If you can begin working on a project before grant guidelines have been published, you have a head start on most of your competitors. Ultimately, you want the grantmaker to turn to you as a resource person who can provide information from the field to help shape the specifics of new grantmaking programs.

As the meeting moves toward its conclusion, leave the grantmaker some information about your organization: a current annual report, a list of your board of trustees, a description of your services, and perhaps a recent newsletter or news release about an exciting event or development. If your organization is currently involved in a building project, you might include a drawing or photograph; if you have achieved impressive results in improving your service record, you can include a graph or table documenting it.

The most important action item in this meeting is to alert your grantmaker that you definitely intend to develop a concept and seek financial support for it. Your goal is to pave the way for a discussion of your project before submitting a proposal. Ideally, the grantmaker will invite you to meet again when you have a specific project in mind. Or the grantmaker might agree to discuss a project by phone when your idea has been fleshed out.

As mentioned in Chapter Four, any get-acquainted meeting can, at a moment's notice, turn into a get-down-to-business meeting. In case this happens, your preparation should always include thinking through one or more specific projects that can be presented if necessary.

The Get-Down-to-Business Meeting

In this type of meeting, the conversation proceeds from the topics of the get-acquainted meeting to a discussion of a specific project. Ideally, the outcome is the grantmaker's inviting you to submit a proposal requesting financial support for the project.

Because this meeting includes a discussion of a project you hope to get funded, the participants should include someone who can speak knowledgeably about it. Sometimes the visionary executive director has conceived the project and can speak eloquently about how it will unfold; in other cases, the project will be beyond the executive's scope and you will need to involve the staff member who will be responsible for implementation.

Conducting the Meeting. The discussion of key issues facing your organization can segue quite naturally into the discussion of a specific project you are seeking to fund. In the case of the hospice program, for example, it was easy to proceed from a discussion of the growing number of children and families requiring hospice care to the desirability of establishing such a service.

Ideally, the grantmaker will offer to review a draft of your proposal and provide guidance in this early stage of your project. This obviously adds a step to the process and forces you to prepare your proposal more quickly in order to leave time for review and revision before the general proposal submission deadline. There is, however, no better investment of your time and effort! Any inconvenience will be more than offset by a quantum leap in your chances of securing a grant, because through the review process the grantmaker becomes an active, collaborative partner in your project; what once was exclusively *your* project has become a *mutual* undertaking.

In either this meeting or the next (when the draft proposal is reviewed), you can look to the grantmaker to suggest which aspects of the project to emphasize and what specific information to include in your proposal. To demonstrate your attitude of respectful receptiveness, all the grantmaker's suggestions should be received gratefully and implemented as promptly as possible—even if it entails a lot of work.

The simple truth, as we have suggested before, is that there is no magic bullet, no secret formula for getting grants. People who believe in instant success buy lottery tickets; the rest of us resign ourselves to hard work. At times, you may be tempted to think that your grantmaker's purpose is merely to create more work for you or to make your task more difficult. You will do far better if you assume that the grantmaker is simply trying to help—which is indeed the case more often than not. Remember, the grantmaker is just as interested as you are in seeing worthwhile projects succeed. No matter how difficult it may be, persist in thinking of the grantmaker as your helper and colleague, not as your adversary.

[Guerrilla] forces should have a strict discipline, a high morale, and a clear comprehension of the task to be performed, without conceit, without illusions, without false hopes of an easy triumph.

CHE GUEVARA, *GUERRILLA WARFARE*

CHAPTER SEVEN

PREPARING AND SUBMITTING YOUR GRANT PROPOSAL

The fundamental principle is that no battle, combat, or skirmish is to be fought unless it will be won.

CHE GUEVARA, GUERRILLA WARFARE

As mentioned earlier, the art of grantsmanship is permeated by myths. Two of the most dangerous ones have to do with proposals.

Myth Number One: When you want to get a grant, the first thing to do is to write a proposal.

Myth Number Two: The quality of the proposal determines whether a grant is awarded.

By now, you know that when you want to get a grant, the first thing to do is to begin a dialogue with a grantmaker; furthermore, the quality of your proposal is less important than the quality of that dialogue and of the relationship on which it's based. In real life, well-crafted proposals are often turned down and even poorly crafted proposals sometimes result in grants. Not that proposals are unimportant, but you need to keep them in perspective.

Preparing a formal proposal requires a significant investment of time, energy, and resources. Before you begin, therefore, assess your chances of winning an award and decide on that basis whether it is worthwhile to submit a proposal. Go forward only if you are convinced that your chances are good. Otherwise, focus on opportunities that are more promising. Remember, you aren't making this decision blindly; you have numerous opportunities to pick up promising or discouraging signals in your conversations, correspondence, and meetings with the grantmaker.

In this chapter, we define the conditions under which it is worthwhile or not worthwhile to prepare a proposal and explain how to obtain maximum benefit for your organization from the process of proposal preparation. Many people see the process as requiring specialized skills and arcane knowledge, but it is really quite straightforward, albeit very time-consuming.

Contrary to popular belief, proposals for government funds are not fundamentally different from proposals to private foundations. Though it is true that government agencies often have more technical requirements than private foundations, nothing that any government agency requires is beyond the grasp of a well-educated layperson. Remember, if public money is being awarded, it is, in a sense, *your* money. As a taxpayer, you have as much right to go after it as any other taxpayer. You can demand that the instructions be explained so that you understand them!

Seven Preliminary Scenarios

Before delving into the details of proposal preparation, let's review seven scenarios that represent the range of preliminary exchanges between grantseeker and grantmaker and suggest the best course of action for each in regard to the preparation of a proposal.

When Is It Worthwhile to Prepare a Proposal?

There are three circumstances in which it is worthwhile to prepare a proposal:

- When you have reason to believe that it will result in the immediate or eventual awarding of a grant
- When you are looking for a way to expedite the planning of a project
- When you wish to open a dialogue and the awarding of a grant is secondary

In the first case, where obtaining a grant is your highest priority, one of three positive scenarios may come into play.

Scenario One: The Optimal. The optimal scenario is to be told by your grantmaker that funds have already been earmarked for your organization and that if you prepare and submit a proposal documenting the agreement you have reached verbally, an award will be made. This is not an everyday occurrence in the world of fundraising, but it does happen (more often with government funding sources than private ones). When it happens, rejoice—and then get to work on the writing!

Scenario Two: High Level of Promise. If the grantmaker initiates a conversation in which you are clearly invited to submit a request, your chances of being awarded a grant are high and you can approach the task of preparing a proposal with great optimism.

Scenario Three: Good Level of Promise. The odds of your being awarded a grant may also be favorable if you initiate the contact and the grantmaker responds to your inquiry with enthusiasm, inviting you explicitly or implicitly to submit a proposal.

When obtaining a grant is a secondary concern, two other positive scenarios are possible.

Scenario Four: Expediting the Planning Process. The fourth scenario prevails when your highest priority is to expedite your internal planning process. An imminent proposal submission deadline may be one of the best tools in your motivational arsenal, helping you to marshal your resources and get people moving quickly. As Boswell's Johnson pointed out, "Depend upon it, sir, when a man knows he is to be hanged in a fortnight, it concentrates his mind wonderfully."[1] The same may be said of an imminent proposal deadline.

Scenario Five: Opening a Dialogue. You may find yourself in a situation where you recognize that you need to build a relationship with a grantmaker but it proves impossible to make the initial contact directly by phone, preliminary letter, or personal visit. You may feel, and it may indeed be the reality, that the only avenue open to you is to submit a proposal. The odds of your receiving a grant in response to a "cold" proposal are slim, but if you view a proposal as the opening gambit in a dialogue you hope to establish—and if on this basis alone you can afford the time, energy, and resources required to prepare it—it may be worth proceeding.

When Is It Not Worthwhile to Prepare a Proposal?

It is generally not worthwhile to prepare a proposal if you find yourself in one of the two following situations.

Scenario Six: Unenthusiastic Response. Let's say that you initiate a contact with a grantmaker and describe your idea either in a conversation or in writing, and the response lacks enthusiasm and interest. In this case, it is probably a waste of time to prepare a proposal, as the chances of being awarded a grant are very slight.

Scenario Seven: No Prior Contact. If your sole purpose is to secure a grant from a particular funder at a particular time, and you have had no conversation or personal correspondence with her, it is probably not worthwhile to submit a proposal.

There seems to be no consensus on what the ratio is between proposals submitted and grants awarded, but various scholars estimate it at somewhere between one in five and one in twenty. Whatever the exact number, we know that grantseeking is a highly competitive activity and that the vast majority of the proposals that result in awards are submitted by people who have had direct contact with the grantmaker.

Preparing a Grant Proposal

If it makes sense to submit a proposal but you have never successfully done so before, you may well be uncertain how best to proceed. The balance of this chapter outlines the steps you should take to obtain the greatest benefit from the process and to maximize your chances of success.

First, the good news: before you embark on the preparation of a proposal, you will have already completed the first step. That is, you will have emerged from the creative struggle of figuring out how to solve a problem or meet a need. You will have generated an idea. This is far and away the most challenging and exciting part of the entire process. Now the bad news: from here on, it is mostly a matter of hard work. However, the method outlined here will enable you to carry out the necessary tasks as efficiently and productively as possible. We discuss in detail the kinds of tasks that must be completed by you, the person in charge of the process, as well as those that can or should be completed by colleagues or other members of your staff.

Sculpting Your Project

The average project is conceived on a fairly abstract level and discussed in a conceptual fashion with grantmakers and perhaps with others. But now it is time to concentrate on making all aspects of the project as concrete as possible.

You might find it helpful to think of this process as mental sculpting. You have the basic materials and a general idea of what you want the finished product to look like; now you will shape the project and add detail to prepare it for exhibition before a select, sophisticated, and demanding audience. On a mundane level, of course, your purpose is to describe in a persuasive fashion the activities that will be part of your project; but even this is a creative process, so bring your creative faculties into play. If you are a verbal thinker, you can develop a list of phrases to describe your project. If you are a visual thinker, you can envision a series of scenes. If you are familiar with the technique of storyboarding, you can use it to illustrate how you believe events will unfold as your project becomes a reality.

Very few grantseekers get dressed, go to their offices, sit down at their desks, and sculpt their projects. The process requires less creativity than generating ideas, but your subconscious can still play a role. You can mull over your project while you do other, less mentally taxing things such as showering, driving, or cooking (but please be careful when mulling while driving or cooking!). Your project will develop organically, evolving as you live with the idea until one day you recognize its proper shape and direction. Given the evolutionary nature of project development, you will be able to carry on other activities that will advance the preparation of your proposal during the days or weeks it takes to reach the final state.

Examining the Criteria for Eligibility

As indicated earlier, the first task that can be conducted on a preliminary basis is determining whether your organization meets the criteria for eligibility established by the grantmaker.

Some requirements, such as tax-exempt status, are almost universal. Only about 5 percent of all grantmaking organizations award grants to individuals. The other 95 percent require that recipients be qualified by the Internal Revenue Service (IRS) as charitable tax-exempt organizations, according to Section 501(c)(3) of the Internal Revenue Code.[2] Other requirements are peculiar to specific funders. Some, for example, require that an organization be in operation for three years before it can be eligible.

Planning the Work

Once you have determined that your organization is eligible for a grant, review the funder's proposal guidelines and map out a plan for preparing all the sections that will eventually be assembled into the document you submit.

Word processing, spreadsheet, and project management software may make it easier for you to do the work in the sequence that makes the most sense and then cut and paste it all together in the order in which it needs to be presented. What information do grantmakers request? In what order do they want it presented, and how much detail do they want to see?

The guidelines published by The Cleveland Foundation, the oldest and second-largest community foundation in the United States, are fairly typical (see Exhibit 7.1).

EXHIBIT 7.1. PROPOSAL GUIDELINES
OF THE CLEVELAND FOUNDATION.

Section One: Your Agency's Background

- Mission
- Founding date
- Major programs
- Links with similar organizations
- Number and capacity of staff

Section Two: The Project You Propose

- The specific community need or policy issue you will address, or
- The contribution your project will make to the community
- Your project's goals and objectives
- The activities you propose to tackle the problem
- Why your organization wants to do the work
- Why your plan is cost-effective
- Expected immediate and long-term results
- Other providers of this service in the Cleveland area
- Distinctive features of your project
- Expected contribution to knowledge in the field
- Relationship to your agency's overall program
- Professional support or other evidence of the project's value

Section Three: Your Project Implementation Plan

- Your timeline: steps to be taken, by whom, and when
- How many people, and who, will be served
- Names of cooperating organizations
- Project staff and/or consultants
- Any advisory groups

Section Four: Project Continuation

- If the project is ongoing, your plans to continue after the funding period
- Future funding sources
- Other current funding sources

Section Five: Project Evaluation

- Your criteria for effectiveness
- Methods and schedule for measuring results
- Methods and schedule for short- and long-term evaluation of results
- Who will assess the results

Section Six: Financial Information

- A line-item income and expense budget for the project
- A budget narrative explaining each line item for which you are requesting Cleveland Foundation support
- The amount your organization will contribute to the project
- A list of other foundations or sources to which you have submitted this proposal. Please indicate whether funds have been committed, declined, or are pending.
- Your organization's current annual operating budget. Please note any deficits and describe your plans to correct them.

Source: Guidelines for Grantseekers, The Cleveland Foundation, February 1996. Reproduced by permission of Dr. Susan N. Lajoie, associate director.

The order of information requested in Exhibit 7.1 may be quite different from the order in which you do the work of developing it. You should strongly consider preparing the sections in the following order:

1. Your agency's background (Section One)
2. Project implementation plan (Section Three)
3. Financial information (Section Six)
4. Project evaluation (Section Five)
5. Project continuation (Section Four)
6. The project you propose (Section Two)

The reason for this order is that over a period of several days, weeks, or even months, you will be cogitating about your project—which must be completed before you approach the sixth and final task. In the meantime, you can begin working on the other sections of the document. With the order recommended here, each task will lead organically to the next, and the final document, once assembled in the order the grantmaker requests, will flow and be both cogent and compelling.

Task One: Your Agency's Background

As you assemble the information listed in Section One of Exhibit 7.1 (describing your organization's mission, programs, staff, and the like), you can also be collecting key documents that grantmakers often require as appendices or enclosures:

- Letter from the IRS designating your organization as tax-exempt
- List of members and officers of your board of trustees, including their business affiliations and positions
- Your current annual report
- A current financial statement, preferably audited
- Job descriptions of project personnel

If this is the first proposal your organization has submitted, or the first one in a long time, you can help your organization by setting up a grantseeking file. Place in it copies of all the documents you assemble so they will be readily available to you and your colleagues in the future. If, on the other hand, your organization has submitted successful proposals in the past, and only *your* involvement is new, you may be able to take a shortcut: update information in the grantseeking file that is no longer current, and simply appropriate the other information.

At this stage, you also need to start working with people outside your organization on at least two issues that will be fleshed out later: future funding for the project, and (if the project is collaborative) the nature of the partnership and how it will work.

Future Funding Partners

You may have already given some thought to the long-term financial viability of the project, but many grantseekers do not think about this until their grantmaker insists on it. The earlier you figure out how the project will be sustained after the grant period, the more attractive your project will be to prospective investors and the more likely you will be to secure both the start-up and continuing support you require. If future funders are closely involved in the planning of a project, they are more likely to continue their involvement downstream.

Therefore, if you haven't already done so, now is the time to begin building good relationships with prospective permanent funders, sponsors, and customers. You should inform these people about the plans you are developing, and build their interests into your planning process. This requires an investment of time and energy, but the results it can produce are worth it.

Collaborating Organizations

Your project may involve partner organizations that collaborate on your grantseeking venture and will provide service when the project is implemented. If so, you have probably established some kind of contact with them and inquired in general terms about the possibility of working together. Now it is time to firm up your plans for collaboration. You need to meet with at least one representative of each potential collaborative partner to determine the role each is interested in undertaking and the level of commitment each expects to make.

Developing collaborative relationships is usually worth the time and energy it requires, as many grantmakers today prefer to support collaborative efforts rather than single-organization projects. These funders maintain that collaboration is generally more efficient and more cost-effective than the alternative because they avoid duplication of effort. On the other hand, it usually makes the project planning and organizational requirements far more complex; dealing with multiple sources of information and multiple administrative approvals may make the process seem not just arithmetically but geometrically more complex. Plan accordingly.

Funders today also have rising expectations about grantseekers' advance planning and commitment to collaboration. As recently as a few years ago, some funders accepted letters of support—expressing little more than hearty best wishes—as documentation of involvement. Now, however, most require contracts or at least firm, formal commitments contingent upon the receipt of funds. When organizational resources are being committed, of course, appropriate authorization is required. This almost always involves a good deal of negotiation, which naturally takes time. So if your project involves one or more collaborating organizations, you cannot afford to defer discussions on how the arrangement will work. "Fudging" the details in your grant proposal is no longer an option.

Task Two: Project Implementation Plan

By this time, the evolutionary process of sculpting your project should have produced a list of activities or a series of scenarios. With this information in hand, you can move on to the next task: your project implementation plan.

A method I have developed to accomplish this is to create what I will call a "timeline matrix." In the process of constructing this grid, you will develop the information on the project timeline requested in Section Three of Exhibit 7.1. You will also develop much of the budget information requested in Section Six. In short, you will answer all of the subquestions involved in these megaquestions: Who will do what to whom, with what, at what cost, and by when? How will we all know it's done and how effectively it was done?

To answer these megaquestions, you will need to identify many things.

- All tasks involved in the project
- Who will be responsible for completing each task
- What resources will be employed in completing each task
- What costs will be incurred in employing these resources
- How long it will take to complete each task
- What milestones will indicate the completion of each task
- What measures will be used to evaluate outcomes
- What benchmarks will be established for changes brought about by the project

Developing a Timeline Matrix

Let's say you are developing a marketing project for a performing arts organization, and one activity will be an advertising campaign. You could construct a timeline matrix to spell out exactly how this would be accomplished. First, list all the questions the timeline matrix will address:

- What media will be used in the advertising campaign?
- How will funds be distributed among direct mail, print, radio, television, billboards, and bus cards?
- Which mailing list or lists will be used for direct mail?

- How will mail be sent—bulk rate or first class?
- Who will prepare the mailing?
- What percentage of the ads in print and electronic media will be free public service announcements as opposed to paid ads?
- Which radio and TV stations will attract the audience the organization wants to target?
- How long will each advertisement be?
- At what time of day will the ads be aired?
- Who will compose the ad copy?
- Who will design the graphics?
- Who will reproduce the graphics?
- What items will need to be printed, and how many copies of each will be needed?
- What size audience can each radio and TV station promise?
- Who will perform in the ads?
- Will royalties need to be paid for music used in the ads? If so, how much and to whom?
- How long a commitment will the organization need to make to the advertising media?
- How will the impact of the advertising be measured?
- How will the organization know that this evaluation was impartial and accurate?
- How will the organization analyze the cost-benefit ratio for future planning purposes?

To answer the questions on a timeline matrix and develop a sound plan, you will need to make some decisions based on incomplete information. If you live in a major metropolitan area, for example, it may not be practical to obtain advertising rates for all TV and radio stations. Therefore, you and your colleagues must come to at least a tentative agreement about the scope of the advertising campaign. As soon as you begin this detailed planning, you must make choices— and, as a consequence, limit the potential of your project.

Many issues will arise as you address the questions you have identified and gather the information you need to come up with answers that make sense. When you have finished constructing your timeline matrix, you will have completed much of the planning that needs to be done for your project.

Allocating Resources to Proposal Preparation

Developing your matrix will be easier if you adopt two strategic approaches to preparing your proposal.

First, make sure you budget sufficient time and resources for the planning and research involved. Before you commit to preparing a proposal, consider how much time and what kind of help is available to you. Factor in this information when deciding whether you can realistically meet the deadline under discussion.

Second, your project will be better planned and its implementation will go more smoothly if you involve colleagues in planning and proposal preparation. You probably have several kinds of colleagues who can help in several ways.

Participating colleagues represent disciplines or functions that will be involved in implementing the project. For instance, if you are planning an educational project, you will want to involve teachers; if you are planning a research effort, you will want to involve researchers.

Service colleagues are those who perform duties that support the mission-oriented work of your organization. The advancement function, for example, includes fund development, marketing, public relations, and planning. Another is the fiscal management function, where colleagues could be consulted if you need to know the value of 10 percent of a staff member's time or the cost of his health insurance. If you need to know how much it will cost to produce a brochure, you would ask someone in public relations to help you develop the estimate.

When you involve colleagues in the planning and proposal preparation process, it helps lighten your personal burden. Beyond that, involving those who will be responsible for implementing and supporting the project confers ownership of the venture on them; people who have been involved in planning a project will be motivated to implement it with greater enthusiasm than those who are merely presented with a *fait accompli*.

Most assistance in preparing your timeline matrix may come from your own staff, but you may need to go outside your organization as well. Do not hesitate to ask professionals or vendors to develop bids; remember, everyone in business is concerned about developing new business. The ethical approach to securing bids or estimates at this point is to make it clear that you do not currently have funding in hand for the work you are discussing. To encourage a prompt response, point out that the estimate or bid process is part of your fundraising effort, and that once you do have the funds in hand, you will consider that vendor to provide the product or service on which they are bidding.

An ancillary benefit of preparing proposals is that you often gain additional information that is even more valuable than what you set out to collect. In most instances, for example, you will follow sound business practice and secure at least two or three bids for each major product or service involved in your project. In this process, you also learn which vendors are easiest to work with and which professionals best fit the culture and style of your organization. Preliminary contact and working together is like courtship and marriage; a date who exhibits bad table manners probably won't improve merely by becoming a husband, and a vendor who fails to return phone calls promptly as you make initial inquiries probably will not improve by being chosen a project implementer.

The timeline matrix you develop will provide the information you need to prepare two key sections of your proposal: the timeline (for Section Three) and the budget (for Section Six).

Completing the Project Timeline

The timeline identifies each activity within your project, who will be responsible for completing it, and what period of time it will require. The time scale you specify depends on the nature of your project, but whether you outline events on a week-by-week or quarter-by-quarter basis, what counts is to demonstrate that you understand all of these:

- What needs to be done
- The order in which tasks need to be accomplished
- How much time this will take
- What resources will be required

Your proposal will have a more professional appearance if you present this information in graphic as well as narrative form. You can do this fairly easily by using project management software to generate a Gantt or PERT (project evaluation and review technique) chart.

Most grantseekers, by the way, significantly underestimate the time required to complete the activities involved in their projects; a good rule of thumb is to double your original estimate. In your project implementation plan, try to accommodate the operation of Murphy's Law: assume things will go wrong. Most grantmakers have extensive experience with a broad range of projects, and if you underestimate the time required to accomplish your goals, they will see you as naive, a poor planner, or both—and that will discourage them from getting involved with you.

Task Three: Financial Information

Many grantmakers agree that they look at the budget first and give it more rigorous scrutiny than any other part of the proposal. If a grantmaker specifies a format for your budget information, follow it. If no format is specified, a template that seems to accommodate most situations is that of The Cleveland Foundation.

Their forms are included as Resource B, and you are welcome to reproduce them.

Before you begin to build your budget, think through all the basic components and parameters of your project:

- Duration of the project
- How much of the project's duration you are asking the funder to support
- Level of resource commitment from your organization
- Number and identity of collaborating organizations and the levels of their resource commitments
- Number and identity of external funders to whom you are applying
- Preferences of specific external funders and any restrictions they will place on the use of funds

Nine Golden Rules

As you plan your budget, you can make it more attractive to funders by applying the nine golden rules of budget building.

Rule One: Keep It Simple. Whenever possible, divide the support you request from multiple sources on a percentage basis. Let's say an expense item costs $1,000 and you have four funders equally capable of supporting it and equally likely to do so. Request $250 from each of the four.

Rule Two: Give Yourself Full Credit. Document as high a level of organizational support as you honestly can. Many people fail through mere oversight to credit their organizations for support in the form of standard business operating costs. Every time someone puts in a new toner cartridge, runs a letter through the postage meter, or staples two pieces of paper together, the organization incurs expenses. Give your organization full credit for providing this support. The more of it you can demonstrate, the more committed your organization will appear and the more attractive your project will be to external funders.

Organizational support can be provided in cash, in-kind services, or both. The expenses involved may be direct or indirect. Commitment is most clearly demonstrated by an allocation of cash for direct expenses, such as compensation for an individual hired specifically to work on the project or the purchase of a piece of equipment specifically for use in it. In-kind services normally include services, staff time, supplies, or equipment provided by the organization without reimbursement. The organization, for example, may donate office space to support the project, or the fiscal officer may agree to oversee the project budget in addition to her other responsibilities.

Indirect expenses may also be incurred. These include overhead or administrative costs that are necessary to the functioning of the project but do not support direct service to clients. Indirect costs are often funded through a donation of in-kind services by the sponsoring organization.

To determine whether organizational resources should be considered cash or in-kind services, ask yourself if you expect a check to be cut specifically for a given expenditure. If you do, that expense probably involves a cash commitment. If you do not expect a check to be cut to cover an expense—such as for 5 percent of the rent or 10 percent of an existing staff person's time—then the commitment is probably in-kind.

Rule Three: Detail the Commitments of Partners. If your project involves one or more collaborating organizations, identify them in your budget and detail their commitment of resources. This demonstrates their level of involvement and their enthusiasm for the project.

Rule Four: Be Specific. Wherever possible, give your budget an aura of specificity by spelling out the number of units and the unit cost before multiplying to come up with a forecasted expense. For instance, if your project involves mailing a newsletter, determine how many copies need to be printed, their unit cost, and the postage cost per copy. Then multiply the unit cost with postage by the number of copies to estimate the total costs of the mailing.

Rule Five: If You Can't Be Specific, Create a Reasonable Fiction. When it is impossible to forecast precisely what something will cost, you can create a reasonable, fact-based fiction. For instance, many funders expect you to be able to forecast exact costs for copying, which is extremely difficult to do. But if you review your organization's expenditures for copying over a recent period, you can probably extrapolate from that to the project you are planning; the number is fictional but reasonable.

Rule Six: Be Prepared for Change. No costs remain static over the life of a project, especially if it lasts more than a year, so allow for inflation and for annual increases in staff compensation. Make sure year-to-year budget projections also reflect any changes in the activities involved in your project; costs increase as you introduce new activities or expand existing activities to serve more people.

Start-up costs should disappear after the first year. Once software has been developed, for example, ongoing maintenance costs can still be included in your budget but the original development cost should be eliminated.

Rule Seven: Nothing Lasts Forever. As discussed previously, though all funders recognize that external support is usually required to get a project up and running, few want to support projects that can never become self-sustaining. Over time, your budget should reflect a diminishing reliance on external funding and an increasing reliance on your own donor base, together with any revenues the project may be able to generate for itself.

Rule Eight: Be Consistent. If you are applying to more than one grantmaker for support, bear in mind that funders are likely to compare notes. They tend to develop their grantmaking strategies in relation to what their counterparts at other foundations or agencies are doing. To maintain your credibility, keep your budget numbers consistent in all the proposals you submit.

Rule Nine: Be Respectful. We all like to think that our organizations are distinctive, even unique, and we are not pleased when others make unwarranted assumptions about us. Grantmakers feel much the same way. Try to respect the limitations of individual funders as you build your budget. For instance, in getting computers paid for, some funders prefer that their money be used to purchase hardware and some prefer that it buy software. If you are aware of such preferences, they should be reflected in the way you build your budget.

Building a Budget: An Example

To illustrate how these guidelines play out in practice, we consider here how one grantseeker built a budget, and the thinking that went into its presentation. You will develop the various sections of your budget in much the same way as you do the proposal narrative: doing the work in one sequence but presenting it in another.

Expenses. Accounting convention requires that revenues be listed before expenses. In putting together a proposal budget, however, you need to calculate your expenses first so you can decide how much grant support to request. To do this, use a project expenses form such as that shown in Exhibit 7.2 to begin building your budget. This example has been filled in for a one-year period. If your project will last more than one year, copy the form and do each year separately. When all years have been completed, total them on another form to serve as a summary. As we review each section of Exhibit 7.2, guidelines will be suggested for developing both the line items and the narrative that must accompany the budget.

Personnel Expenses. In estimating the percentage of a person's time allocated to a project, it is usually easiest to think about how much time the individual will spend

EXHIBIT 7.2. PROJECT EXPENSES.

	Percent on Project	Organizational Contribution	Other Funding Sources	Cleveland Foundation Request	Total
Personnel Expenses					
Staff Costs					
Position title					
Executive Director	60%	$_____	$ 13,500	$ 16,500	$ 30,000
Administrative Assistant	40%	$_____	$ 4,500	$ 5,500	$ 10,000
_____	___%	$_____	$_____	$_____	$_____
_____	___%	$_____	$_____	$_____	$_____
Staff Costs Subtotal		$_____	$ 18,000	$ 22,000	$ 40,000
Fringe Benefits (explain in narrative)		$_____	$ 4,500	$ 5,500	$ 10,000
Fringe Benefits Subtotal		$_____	$ 4,500	$ 5,500	$ 10,000
Total Personnel Expenses		$_____	$ 22,500	$ 27,500	$ 50,000
Non-Personnel Expenses					
Contract Services					
Consultants		$_____	$ 15,750	$ 19,250	$ 35,000
Legal services		$_____	$ 1,080	$ 1,320	$ 2,400
Temporary services		$_____	$_____	$_____	$_____
Audit services		$_____	$_____	$_____	$_____
Other (explain in narrative)		$_____	$_____	$_____	$_____
Contract Services Subtotal		$_____	$ 16,830	$ 20,570	$ 37,400
Office Space					
Rent		$ 14,400	$_____	$_____	$ 14,400
Utilities		$ 960	$_____	$_____	$ 960
Furnishings		$_____	$_____	$_____	$_____
Maintenance		$_____	$_____	$_____	$_____
Insurance		$ 1,200	$_____	$_____	$ 1,200
Other (explain in narrative)		$_____	$_____	$_____	$_____
Office Space Subtotal		$ 16,560	$_____	$_____	$ 16,560
Equipment/Supplies					
Office Supplies		$_____	$ 128	$ 155	$ 283
Printing		$_____	$ 653	$ 797	$ 1,450
Postage and delivery		$_____	$ 225	$ 275	$ 500
Copier rental/supplies		$_____	$ 338	$ 412	$ 750
Telephone/fax (local/long distance)		$_____	$ 1,899	$ 2,321	$ 4,220
Repairs/maintenance		$_____	$ 0	$ 0	$ 0
Computer supplies/maintenance		$_____	$ 0	$ 14,850	$ 14,850
Other (explain in narrative)		$_____	$ 23,373	$ 0	$ 23,373
Equipment/Supplies Subtotal		$_____	$ 26,615	$ 18,810	$ 45,425

EXHIBIT 7.2. PROJECT EXPENSES, cont'd.

	Organizational Contribution	Other Funding Sources	Cleveland Foundation Request	Total
Travel Related Expenses				
Air travel	$_____	$_____	$_____	$_____
Out-of-town expenses	$_____	$_____	$_____	$_____
In-town expenses (parking/mileage)	$_____	$_____	$_____	$_____
Meetings/seminars/conference fees	$_____	$_____	$_____	$_____
Other (explain in narrative)	$_____	$_____	$_____	$_____
Travel Related Expenses Subtotal	$_____	$_____	$_____	$_____
Other				
Indirect cost (explain in narrative)	$_____	$_____	$_____	$_____
Volunteer Recognition Banquet	$_____	$ 3,000	$_____	$ 3,000
_____	$_____	$_____	$_____	$_____
Other Subtotal	$_____	$ 3,000	$_____	$ 3,000
Total Non-Personnel Expenses	$_____	$ 29,615	$ 18,810	$ 48,425
TOTAL PROJECT EXPENSES	$_____	$_____	$_____	$_____

Requesting Organization: Cleveland Rape Crisis Center

Prepared By: Mary Brigid

Phone Number: (216) 555-3914

Format used by permission of Dr. Susan N. Lajoie, associate director, The Cleveland Foundation. Sample budget adapted from the Capacity-Building Project of the Cleveland Rape Crisis Center and used by permission of Mary Brigid, executive director.

on a weekly basis and then multiply by fifty-two. For people who will be spending a major portion of their time on the project, you can base your calculations on a total of 2,080 paid work hours in the year.

Consult your fiscal office to obtain information on fringe benefits. Be sure to ask what costs are covered, as these vary considerably from one organization to another, and even from one position to another.

Nonpersonnel Expenses. Contract services, especially consultants, can present problems in a review by a program officer. Because foundations generally base their own payments to consultants on the government rate, program officers who scrutinize your proposal may not be well informed about current market rates. You are well advised to contact a national organization in the consultant's field of expertise and request a written statement that documents the generally accepted market rates in the field. If you cannot obtain a written statement, at least discuss the matter with an objective third party and take some notes on what market rates are perceived to be. To determine a consulting fee, you will need either the consultant's estimated total fee, or an hourly or daily rate plus the consultant's estimate of the amount of time the job will require.

Your project may or may not involve other contract services. If it does, be sure to retain the worksheets in which your estimate was developed—hourly rate and number of hours—to review with your grantmaker during a meeting after the proposal is submitted.

Office Space. You may have given minimal thought to some line items, such as the cost of insurance or utilities. Wherever costs are unknown to you, work with your business office staff to do the research and estimate the numbers.

Equipment and Supplies. It's very difficult to forecast many of these line items. The best method is to prorate your organization's annual expenditures based on the relationship of your project to the rest of the organization's activities.

Travel and Related Expenses. Because so many scandals and abuses have involved the inappropriate use of grant, government, or nonprofit funds, this section will be very closely scrutinized. To make sure your budget holds up, be extra careful when estimating any travel expenses for which you are seeking support. Hotel and airline rates change frequently and sometimes dramatically; when you prepare your budget, you may not know where your professional meetings and conferences will be held two or three years later. Many large organizations book hotel space as far in advance as possible, but smaller organizations may not select a site for a meeting that far ahead. If that is the case:

- Review your actual travel costs for the past few years.
- Select a few representative meeting sites. Contact a travel agent to determine the current travel and hotel costs for these sites.
- Hope that the organization doesn't select a site that is much more distant or a hotel that is much more expensive.

Revenues. When you have finished estimating your project expenses, you can move on to the next section of the budget: project revenues. In the Exhibit 7.3 example, the format requires you to distinguish between funds that are committed and those that are anticipated. Under "Committed Funds," list only those grants for which you have a written, legally binding commitment. Organizational income may be challenging to forecast; you will usually be close if you review your organization's budget history and base your calculations on the trends of the past several years.

EXHIBIT 7.3. PROJECT REVENUES.

THE CLEVELAND FOUNDATION
PROJECT BUDGET REQUEST

(Please copy form for multiple-year projects)

Requesting Organization: Cleveland Rape Crisis Center

Project Title: Capacity Building Project

Project Duration: **From** 1/1/98   **To** 2/28/98

Total amount requested from The Cleveland Foundation: $ 66,680

PROJECT REVENUES

Grants and other support

	Committed	Anticipated	Total
Government			
City	$_____	$_____	$_____
County	$_____	$_____	$_____
State	$_____	$_____	$_____
Federal	$_____	$_____	$_____
Government Subtotal	$_____	$_____	$_____
Foundations and Corporations (list separately)			
The Cleveland Foundation	$_____	$ 66,680	$ 66,680
The George Gund Foundation	$_____	$ 45,505	$ 45,505
The Bruening Foundation	$_____	$ 23,441	$ 23,441
_____	$_____	$_____	$_____
Foundations and Corporations Subtotal	$_____	$ 135,626	$ 135,626
Organizational Income			
Membership fees/dues	$_____	$_____	$_____
Contract services	$_____	$_____	$_____
Fundraising events	$_____	$_____	$_____
Other	$_____	$_____	$_____
Organizational Income Subtotal	$_____	$_____	$_____
Other (specify)			
_____	$_____	$_____	$_____
_____	$_____	$_____	$_____
Other Subtotal	$_____	$_____	$_____
TOTAL PROJECT REVENUES	$_____	$_____	$_____
In-Kind (List below: *do not* include in total)			
Office Space/Utilities	$ 15,360	$_____	$ 15,360
Insurance	$ 1,200	$_____	$ 1,200
_____	$ 16,560	$_____	$ 16,560

Format used by permission of Dr. Susan N. Lajoie, associate director, The Cleveland Foundation. Sample budget adapted from the Capacity-Building Project of the Cleveland Rape Crisis Center and used by permission of Mary Brigid, executive director.

From the revenue section of your budget, you draw the information to use in the project budget request. For obvious reasons, most grantmakers are more interested in the funds you are requesting from *them* than the funds you are seeking elsewhere. Prior to any meeting or conversation with them regarding budgets, review your backup material; when you discuss the funds you are seeking from them, be prepared to discuss in detail the reasoning behind each line item.

With all this detail completed, you are now in a position to prepare a budget summary like the one in Exhibit 7.4. The numbers in a budget summary should be taken directly from the budget detail and be consistent throughout your budget sheets. If you use spreadsheet software to develop your budget, your numbers will be subject to rounding; be sure to review all sums manually so you can correct the effects of rounding, because you can be sure that your grantmaker will check your math manually. Any errors, even those produced by automatic rounding, can damage your credibility.

Budget Narrative. The grantmaker may suggest the level of detail grantseekers should include in the budget narrative. Following are two of The Cleveland Foundation's examples of detail about expenses for which funding is sought, one for a staff position and one for a nonpersonnel item.

> *Project director:* This position is accountable for planning, organizing, and directing the implementation and operations of the project. Specific responsibilities include directing staff, orientation, training, and evaluation in accordance with department standards. The project director also directly supervises three case managers.
>
> *Postage:* The total requested postage budget is $2,500. This includes mailing routine correspondence, as well as the community health assessment questionnaire. The questionnaire is an integral component of our activities in year one, as outlined on page 22 of our proposal. The total number of questionnaires to be mailed is 7,500, at a cost of $2,175. The $325 balance is for the mailing of routine correspondence.[3]

Task Four: Project Evaluation

By this time, you know more about your project than you probably ever cared to, and you are definitely in the home stretch. Now you need to flesh out the plan for evaluating your project, which will become Section Five of your completed proposal.

EXHIBIT 7.4. A BUDGET SUMMARY.

THE CLEVELAND FOUNDATION
BUDGET SUMMARY

Requesting Organization: Cleveland Rape Crisis Center
Project Title: Capacity Building

SUMMARY OF PROJECT REVENUES

Revenues (committed and anticipated)	
Grants and other support Government	$ _____
Foundations and Corporations	
The Cleveland Foundation	$ 66,880
The George Gund Foundation	$ 45,504
The Bruening Foundation	$ 23,441
_____	$ _____
Foundations and Corporations Subtotal	$ 135,825
Organizational Income	$ _____
Other	$ _____
Total Project Revenues	$ 135,825
In-Kind (not included in total)	$ 16,560

SUMMARY OF PROJECT EXPENSES

Expenses	
Personnel Expenses	
Staff Costs	$ 40,000
Fringes	$ 10,000
Personnel Expenses Subtotal	$ 50,000
Non-Personnel Expenses	
Contract Services	$ 37,400
Office Space	$ 15,360
Equipment/Supplies	$ 45,425
Travel/Related Expenses	$ 0
Other	$ 4,200
Non-Personnel Expenses Subtotal	$ 102,385
Total Project Expenses	$ 152,385

Format used by permission of Dr. Susan N. Lajoie, associate director, The Cleveland Foundation. Sample budget adapted from the Capacity-Building Project of the Cleveland Rape Crisis
Center and used by permission of Mary Brigid, executive director.

You must define the criteria for a successful project, explaining when and how you plan to measure your results, both short-term and long-term, and who will be responsible for the evaluation process. Whenever possible, try to use standard instruments to measure progress. If no one within your organization really understands project evaluation, consult an expert from a university in your area.

Task Five: Project Continuation

If you recall, at the outset you were encouraged to pursue discussions with future funders, beneficiaries of your services, and members of other key constituencies in order to incorporate their interests into your planning and proposal preparation process. And in developing your budget projections, you were encouraged to show progressively less dependence on external sources of funding over time.

To complete the task of preparing Section Four of your proposal, provide as much detail as you can on how you plan to continue the project after the termination of the grant. Refer to projected budget revenues and explain how each source of committed funds and anticipated funds will contribute to the ongoing support of the project. These may include increased support from your own donor base as well as any revenues generated by the project.

Task Six: Project Description

Strange as it may sound, this moment late in the process is truly the best time to develop your statement of need, which will become Section Two of your proposal describing in detail the problem you are hoping to solve or the issue you are planning to address. Here, you also explain your project's goals and objectives and provide other information you may have skipped over in your first pass. Show how your project goals relate to your organization's overall mission, purpose, and long-range plan.

Why formulate your goals and objectives after your timeline and budget? Because only then will you have thought through what you are really going to do! You will not be indulging in vague rhetoric, as so many grantseekers do, but making definite statements that can be fully supported by all the detailed information you developed in the course of completing the previous tasks. At this point, of course, your goals and objectives should clearly reflect the activities you are going to conduct, including evaluation of the project.

Final Steps

Once the proposal narrative and budget are completed, you can move on to the part of the package that, next to the budget, will get the most attention: the executive summary. You also need to prepare a cover letter and assemble letters of support, and it all has to be done by the deadline.

Executive Summary

Preparing this is one of the most challenging tasks a writer can be assigned. In a few hundred words you must summarize, in a coherent and persuasive fashion, the most important points you have made in the six sections of your proposal and give the reader the sense that your project deserves full attention and close consideration. Faced with this challenge, many grantseekers resort to vague generalizations; others struggle to include as many facts as possible. Neither is ideal. A better approach is to try to select those significant few facts that best support the major points you want to get across. Be sure to leave plenty of time to perform this task. As Pascal once noted: "The present letter is a very long one simply because I had no leisure to make it shorter."[4]

Most grantmakers do specify a length limit for this section, and it should be strictly observed. Sometimes grantseekers succumb to the temptation to reduce the size of the type they are using in order to cram in more copy, rather than editing the contents ruthlessly. This is not a good idea. If a grantmaker has to squint to read it, your document will put her in a bad mood, and if she is in a bad mood, she will be more critical of your document, if she reads it at all. Picture her at 11 P.M. with a big stack of proposals before her. For your own best outcome, be considerate and never use smaller type than twelve-point!

Cover Letter

In your cover letter, you will have even less room for facts or persuasion. You can take a paragraph to describe the nature of your project, its cost, and the amount of the grant you are seeking, which should be mentioned as early as possible. In another paragraph, you can emphasize why you chose to approach this particular grantmaker, and mention the benefits to constituents that will be most important to the grantmaker.

The cover letter should be signed by the officials specified by the grantmaker, usually the chief executive officer and an officer of the board. If they have specific thoughts about the importance of your project, their perspective should be integrated into the letter. If someone else in your organization has had direct contact with the grantmaker, try to dream up a clever way to refer to this person so the grantmaker can identify more closely with your organization.

Letters of Support or Participation

You may be aware that many proposals include letters of support and that you need to secure them and include them before your proposal can be submitted. Your first inclination—especially if you work in a large organization—would be to approach the head of the department in which the grant is being sought, or the CEO of your organization. Although securing letters from these individuals is the easiest path, using such letters gives the grantmaker the wrong impression. At best, it makes your organization appear either self-serving or arrogant; at worst, it makes your organization appear as one in which cooperation and collaboration are so rare that cases of people working together merit documentation.

The people on whom you should concentrate, rather, are *external partners* in a collaborative project, or *outside experts* in your field.

The best way to secure good letters from people external to your organization is to follow the procedure we will outline here, a procedure which recognizes that it is unlikely that the people who head organizations and need to sign the letters will be able to draft them within your time constraints, which usually means within a day or two at most. Remember, no matter how enthusiastic they may be, your project is probably not nearly as important to *them* as it is to *you*. Also, you probably know your project much better than they do—which means that it is easier for *you* to draft a letter which is relevant to your project than it is for *them*.

To ensure that you receive the letters you need in a timely fashion, therefore, and that they are as accurate as possible, you can get what you need and enhance your relationships with colleagues in the process, if you follow these steps:

1. Call the person whom you are asking to sign the letter. Explain that you would appreciate having a letter of support (or participation) for a project you are seeking to fund.
2. To make it as easy as possible for her to comply with your request, offer to provide a draft of the letter.
3. Once she indicates that she is willing to sign a letter, make arrangements to send her the draft. If you are sending the draft on a computer disk, make sure to inquire about compatibility of word processing software, and be sure you exchange accurate addresses to accommodate the requirements of the mode of transmission, whether it be the postal service, overnight delivery service, or electronic mail.
4. Draft the letter as you would like it to read. Follow the same principles you applied in writing your proposal: keep it *specific*, and keep it *short*.

The point of going to such lengths is to make the preparation of the letter *as easy as possible* for the person who will be signing it. Ideally, as soon as she receives your draft, her secretary will merely print out the draft on her letterhead, have it signed, and send it back to you.

Sending the Proposal

When you have received all the letters from your collaborating partners or supporting organizations, add them to your proposal packet. At last, it is time to ship the proposal to the grantmaker! Just a few notes about this final step.

If the grantmaker is a government agency, your proposal absolutely, positively must arrive by the deadline specified. Bureaucrats are simply inflexible. If you get caught in a last-minute crunch, as most grantseekers do, be sure to take an additional step just in case the weather prevents your overnight carrier from delivering on time: different carriers have air hubs in different parts of the country, so send a duplicate package by a different carrier. At least one is almost certain to arrive on time. This is cheap insurance! Finally, be sure to mail copies of the completed proposal promptly to your collaborating partners, to help them feel good about your partnership. Also send a copy to your board president or chair.

Benefits of Preparing a Proposal

By keeping the proposal preparation process in its proper perspective—as an element that is necessary but not sufficient to win a grant award—you are in a position to judge when it is worthwhile to commit yourself to the hard work required to prepare a high-quality proposal.

You should also be prepared to approach this complex task in an efficient and effective manner. If you follow the steps outlined here, you accomplish much of the planning required to shape your project, in the process developing and refining many skills that will help you to become a more effective manager: allocating time and resources, collaborating with colleagues and others outside your organization, conducting research, planning, and budgeting. In all these ways, you and your organization benefit from the process of preparing a grant proposal. Most important, you greatly increase your chances of winning an award and advancing the work of your organization.

Bundles of writing materials should not be carried in excess of needs. Normally, two bundles per regiment, one per battalion, and one per company are permissible. The weight of each bundle should not exceed 40 kilograms.

MAO TSE-TUNG, *BASIC TACTICS*

CHAPTER EIGHT

SUCCESSFUL MEETINGS (AFTER SUBMITTING YOUR PROPOSAL)

So that they may be able to call upon one another for aid and receive information at all times regarding the situation . . . guerrilla units should do their utmost to maintain the closest and most solid relations with the local population for the exchange of correspondence.

MAO TSE-TUNG, *BASIC TACTICS*

People new to grantseeking tend to see the period after proposal submission as a void, because they do not know how their request is faring. Their anxiety may lead them to imagine the worst (see cartoon on p. 105). Many grantmakers never reveal the details of their proposal consideration processes, but others are more forthcoming and want to discuss the questions that arise from reviewing your proposal. They may invite you to meet with them either at their office or at your site. In either case, apply the same principles of successful meetings outlined in Chapter Six.

Office Visits

In some cases, your grantmaker will share specific concerns prior to the meeting so you can prepare accordingly. If not, prepare in a more general way. The best strategy is to prepare yourself to address those areas that frequently prompt questions.

Addressing Problem Areas

The area that usually gets the closest scrutiny and raises the greatest number of questions is the budget. So expect to be asked how you decided what it will cost to implement the project, and why you made the decisions you did. In preparing to defend your budget, the key is to document all the assumptions that went into building it:

- How many hours did you estimate it would take a specific person to complete a specific task?
- On what basis did you calculate the amount of time you estimated?
- What is each individual's hourly rate of compensation? What rate was used to calculate fringe benefits?
- On what basis did you estimate travel costs?
- Did you secure competitive bids for equipment?
- What rate was used to calculate overhead costs?

If the staff members who prepared the budget will be participating in the meeting, they should review their worksheets and be prepared to explain their thought processes. If these people will not be participating, they should thoroughly brief those who will.

Another area that frequently gives rise to questions is the implementation plan, which details who is going to do what, to whom, with what, by when. Your project director should have at his fingertips a detailed justification of why each task was assigned and described as it was in your proposal. You should also be able to explain the reasoning behind the selection of specific milestones.

A third area that sometimes needs defending is the statement of need. If your project director did not prepare this statement himself, he should be brought up to speed on all the sources used in preparing it, the scope of the literature search conducted, or the experience base the author drew on in developing the statement.

A fourth area that prompts questions is the project evaluation. If you hastily sketched out a plan for evaluating the effectiveness of your project, you would be wise to develop a more detailed plan for your postsubmission meeting.

When you have assembled all this information, you have probably done all you can to prepare yourself for the meeting. Now concentrate on the strategies you can use to persuade the grantmaker that your project is superior to its competitors.

To accomplish this, you will need to convey seven winning messages to the grantmaker.

Seven Winning Messages

Message one: This project is important. It will make a difference.

To convey this message, go back to the very beginning and think about the change that you set out to make when you first developed your project concept.

WHEN GRANTSEEKERS IMAGINE THE WORST.

WE HAVE READ YOUR PROPOSAL AND ARE GIVING IT SERIOUS CONSIDERATION

Grantmakers see their grant awards as catalysts for change, so your job is to demonstrate—in quantifiable terms, if at all possible—the ways the world will be a different place once your project is implemented. Will fewer children starve? Will your city's tax base be improved? Will the incidence of cancer be reduced? Will fewer husbands beat their wives? In essence, you need to clearly define the benefits of your project.

Message two: We have thought through all the thorny planning issues; we may not have solved them all yet, but we have developed a strategy or a plan for handling each one.

To convey this message, conduct a thorough analysis of what it will take to implement your project. The following anecdote illustrates the kind of thinking that is necessary.

True Story

The Center for the Prevention of Domestic Violence in Cleveland was struggling with the challenge of reducing domestic violence. In the late 1980s, the center realized that most programs in the field provided services only to victims, ignoring perpetrators;

historically, perpetrators had demonstrated great reluctance to participate in counseling. The organization began seeking grant support to start a program for perpetrators. The executive director impressed the grantmaker by acknowledging the problem, and by sharing with her several strategies that had been developed to attract perpetrators to counseling. The center planned to try these strategies in priority order. If one failed, then alternatives were available.

Not all problems must be solved before you approach a grantmaker, but you should at least be able to indicate that you are aware of the problems and thinking about solutions that seem likely to work.

Message three: I will deliver.

This is the most crucial message of all. We have mentioned it before, but the importance of following through cannot be overstated. All the great ideas, all the impressive research, all the detailed planning will mean nothing if you fail to follow through, if you cannot be counted on to do what you say you are going to do.

There are two ways to convince your grantmaker that you will deliver: cite past instances when you delivered as promised, and deliver as promised now. For instance, if the grantmaker asks a question, and you do not have the answer, you should promise to get it and then do so in a timely fashion. Or if a grantmaker makes the suggestion that you consider the findings or ideas of a certain researcher, look it up promptly and think about how it might apply; then call the grantmaker with thanks for the suggestion and a description of how you will incorporate your new insights.

Message four: I will be easy to work with.

The quality of a working relationship is important, and this includes how well you get along with people. Grantmakers, like everyone else, prefer to work with people who are agreeable, show initiative, comply with guidelines, and do not argue.

People who are judged easy to work with understand the power structure and work within it. Some grantseekers may consider this "selling out," but the successful ones merely accept it as pragmatic; in today's highly competitive environment, no grantmaker has to put up with a grantseeker who causes hassles.

Message five: I really know what I am doing.

Everything you do and everything you say to the grantmaker contributes to the impression that you know what you are doing (or the unfortunate opposite). An impression of knowledge and competence is created by behaving in a businesslike manner; by demonstrating your diligence; and by showing that you are willing to do whatever it takes to satisfy the grantmaker.

Message six: We are committed to moving ahead, whether or not the grant is awarded.

Your grantmaker must be convinced that your project has grown out of a deep institutional commitment such that you will move forward with or without the grant. If the grantmaker thinks you are submitting a proposal just because grant funds are available, you will be perceived as a mere opportunist who is only in it for the money and thus probably unworthy of an award. No grantmaker wants to fund a project that may be abandoned as soon as the grant money runs out.

Message seven: The grant is crucial to the advancement of this project.

This presents a real challenge: the grantmaker must be convinced that you are committed to implementing your project, and at the same time persuaded that you really need external support to carry it out! If you appear too independent and self-sufficient, the grantmaker may feel her support is less than essential and may be less inclined to give you an award.

Messages six and seven truly are logically contradictory. Nevertheless, you need to convey both simultaneously to secure a grant. Striking a balance is a delicate operation, but you might try finessing the situation by affirming that your organization is deeply committed to the project but indicating that without grant support it will be implemented more slowly—that if you raise less money than you want, fewer people will be served, and the project will have less impact.

Selecting the Participants

At the postsubmission meeting, your organization should be represented by the project director or principal investigator, and by any others he may designate. Whether you need the continued participation of your CEO and volunteer leader depends on the project and the size and complexity of your organization, but if they are willing to participate, they should be encouraged to do so.

If your project is collaborative, a representative of each collaborating organization should participate. Select someone as high in the organization as possible to demonstrate the partner's institutional commitment.

Conducting the Meeting

At the meeting, your first priority is to answer all the questions posed by the grantmaker. In the process, you will have opportunities to present your case and to convey the seven winning messages; do your best to weave this into your responses without preempting the grantmaker's agenda.

The meeting also provides an opportunity to secure some detailed information about the grantmaking process—the kind of information that is rarely, if ever, published. It is legitimate for you to ask about all these details:

- When proposals will be reviewed
- What process the program officer will use in recommending proposals for funding
- Who will review the proposals after the program officer completes her review
- How and when the award decisions will be made

This discussion should take place in the context of building the relationship. You want to enlist the grantmaker as your advocate in the deliberation process and provide all the ammunition she needs to make the case for your project. Given that successful grantseekers view grantmakers as allies rather than adversaries, assume that the program officer wants to be supportive and will present your case as convincingly as possible to colleagues, trustees, and others participating in the decision-making process. Your job is to make sure she has any information that might help her to represent you more effectively.

Site Visits

Because the grantmaker is your customer, meetings will be held at the location of her choice. Most often, she will prefer her own office, which saves her time and trouble. On some occasions, however, the grantmaker will want to meet with you in your native habitat. These site visits can range from short informal meetings to extended formal sessions.

Informal site visits normally last one or two hours and involve only one or two representatives of the grantmaking organization. If one of these representatives is the program officer, the impressions gleaned from the visit will help shape her recommendations to the decision makers at her organization.

Formal site visits may last as long as two days. They may involve a team of experts recruited by the grantmaking organization for the specific purpose of making such visits. The program officer may not be included, in which case the people with whom you must interact are important intermediaries and you operate at two levels of separation from the decision makers. It is imperative for you to create a singular and focused impression, as it may well be distorted as it passes through two levels of filters.

The principles to apply in planning and conducting site visits are the same as those of other kinds of meetings, with a few added dimensions:

- Hospitality and (more or less) informal time together, providing greater opportunities to converse and get acquainted
- The opportunity for the grantmaker to visit your facilities, observe your services in action, and perhaps have some informal contact with your clients

The outcome you seek is to convince your visitors that your project merits support and that your application should move ahead in the competition.

Selecting the Participants

When inviting people to make presentations at site visits, exercise restraint even if you are planning an extended formal visit. If planning a two-day visit, for example, you may be tempted to involve a large number of individuals in the hope of demonstrating a broad base of involvement and support. Although your key constituencies should be represented, remember that quality is always more important than quantity. A few well-chosen individuals who are enthusiastic and involved will make a better impression than a cast of thousands that includes people who are vague about the details of your project or whose interest is only political.

As in other meetings, consider inviting your project director or principal investigator, CEO or staff leader, board chair or volunteer leader, representatives of all collaborating organizations, and co-funders. These are often very busy people with overcommitted schedules, and if they develop a schedule conflict they may ask if they can designate someone else to represent them. Unless you know and have worked with the designee, you should politely decline; a last-minute stand-in usually cannot speak as knowledgeably and often lacks the eloquence or presentation skills of the principal.

Developing the Agenda

A formal site visit requires a written agenda. As usual, the grantmaker decides which of you is responsible for developing the agenda. If the grantmaker is responsible, you will need to spend some time studying the agenda to infer her priorities for the visit, based on the order and weighting of topics.

If you build the agenda, keep in mind that your visitors are coming to discuss the project and to enter into a dialogue, not to view a "song-and-dance routine." Be sure to leave time for interaction and discussion, rather than planning a presentation that fills every available minute. Also, allow for the variation in quality of your speakers. You can use scheduling to maximize the impact of your best speakers; use them first and last, or before and after a break, to make the best impression: people are most attentive at the beginning of a meeting and also tend to remember the last thing they hear.

Planning a Site Visit Agenda: An Example

Project Background

In seeking funds to renovate an 80–year-old residential facility, the YMCA of Cleveland learned of an opportunity to secure grant funding from the U.S. Department of Housing and Urban Development (HUD). The HUD funding would pay for renovation as part of a transitional housing program designed to help homeless mentally ill men become independent.

Such a program was deemed well within the mission of the YMCA, even though it did not have staff trained to provide all the services needed by such a client population. In the project that was developed, the Y would provide housing and fitness programming and neighboring organizations would provide other program elements: case management, counseling, employment training, inpatient detoxification, and chemical dependency counseling. The project was called Y-Haven.

Planning for the Visit

The planning team wanted to show the visiting HUD team that a grant would enable it to convert existing space into appropriate facilities for the population to be served, and that the assembled service team had the capacity to provide services effectively. The site visit, however, was scheduled to be completed in only four hours. Exhibit 8.1 shows the agenda the planners developed.

This meeting involved a fairly large number of participants because of the need to include collaborating organizations and co-funders. In the segment on program operation, the CEOs of the collaborating organizations discussed the role their organizations expected to play in the project.

Rather than having the meals component of the program recited to them, during lunch the visitors got a sample of the hot meals program participants would receive. Also at lunch, funders providing money to match the HUD challenge grant discussed their interest in and support of the project.

Because time was extremely limited, volunteer leaders were not invited to address the visitors formally. Instead, they were invited to join the lunch and encouraged to mingle informally.

EXHIBIT 8.1. AGENDA FOR SITE VISIT.

10:00 A.M.	Meet at West Side YMCA, 3200 Franklin Avenue	
10:00–10:10	Welcome and introduction	Clifford A. Smith, president, YMCA
10:10–10:25	Tour of West Side YMCA residential facility	Elving Otero, vice president for development, YMCA
10:25–10:45	Photo exhibit of newly renovated Central YMCA; Q&A on renovation plan	Lee Studer, vice president for facilities, YMCA
10:45–12:00	Program operation: Counseling and case management	Kathy Steinecker, Money & Mailboxes
	Detoxification and chemical dependency counseling	Mary Reed, St. Vincent Charity Health Center
	Employment training	Holly Gigante, Mary Dugan West Side Multi-Service Center
	Empowerment training	Rev. Bob Begin, West Side Ecumenical Ministry
	Fitness training	Jeff Sadowsky, director, YMCA
12:00–12:10 P.M.	Break	
12:10–1:00	Lunch with funding partners and program designers (hot meal provided by Catholic Hunger & Shelter Fund)	
1:00–1:15	Budget review and future funding	
1:15–1:45	Funding partners: The Cleveland Foundation	Goldie Alvis, senior program officer
	The Eva L. and Joseph M. Bruening Foundation	Janet Narten, executive director
	City of Cleveland Department of Development	Christopher Warren, director

Being Hospitable

Whether your visitors are coming from across town or across the country, hospitality plays an important part in the impression you create. As the host, it is up to you to make the trip to your site as easy as possible. As for the selection of a driver, you might be tempted to send a car or a van with a professional driver to transport your visitors, but stop and think a moment. The time your visitors spend going from the airport to the hotel or from the hotel to your site can be used to get acquainted and to discuss your project informally. So select a driver who can help advance the relationship so as to get the maximum benefit during this time. If your visitors are driving, be sure to make arrangements for easy, convenient, and free parking, whatever it takes. If your guests are visiting from out of town, arrange lodging that is as convenient and comfortable as possible without being lavish or ostentatious. It is always gracious to provide meals, snacks, and beverages; these need not be elaborate, but should be prepared specifically for your visitors and presented as nicely as possible.

True Story

A grantmaker spent a day making site visits to two competing organizations. Both had distinguished track records and reputations in their fields.

Organization A had sent the grantmaker its agenda a week before the visit, and she had reviewed it with the principal investigator over the telephone. She also was sent a parking pass that enabled her to park free in a reserved space in a lot adjacent to the meeting site. When she arrived on a warm summer afternoon, she was offered a cold drink and her choice from a platter of fruit and cookies. Participating in the meeting were a key administrator and the appropriate department head, as well as the principal investigator and other staff members responsible for implementing the project.

Prior to the meeting with Organization B, the grantmaker received no advance information and spoke to no one. Arriving for the meeting, she spent fifteen minutes finding a parking space and another twenty minutes hiking from a distant garage to the meeting site. At 11 A.M., picked-over doughnuts from an earlier meeting on the conference room table and reheated coffee were still available, and the project's principal investigator, who along with a graduate student was the only one who could make the meeting, offered them to her.

Guess who got the grant.

Communicating with the Grantmaker

Before and after the site visit, you have many opportunities to communicate with your grantmaker and build your relationship. Beforehand, you can discuss the agenda; if the grantmaker prepares it, you can develop questions, discuss them, and review your plans. If the grantmaker leaves it to you to develop the agenda, share a draft with her so she can review it and determine whether you have adequately addressed her priorities.

Travel is another matter worth discussing before the grantmaker's visit. If your visitor is coming from out of town, send maps, details on transportation, a list of restaurants, and information about sites of interest. Even if visitors are coming from nearby, a detailed map of your site can be helpful.

After the visit, concentrate on following up on any questions that arose. After submitting requested information, call to make sure it has been received and is clear and adequate. In another week or ten days, call again to ask if further information or clarification is needed.

The main difference between a formal and an informal site visit is that the first involves larger numbers of people, a more complex agenda, and more extensive follow-up, and the latter allows you to be more spontaneous.

We have now discussed all four kinds of meetings involving grantseekers and grantmakers. Before your proposal is submitted, you may be invited to participate in a get-acquainted or get-down-to-business meeting; after submitting it you may be invited to a postsubmission meeting at the grantmaker's office or at your site.

There are some differences in how you prepare for and conduct yourself in these various meetings, but the basic principles underlying all interactions between you and the grantmaker remain constant: be attentive to detail, plan carefully, and respond with flexibility and respect.

As Milton Garrett, a wise trustee of the Cleveland Institute of Music, once told me, "People who plan do better than people who don't plan. People who are willing to change their plans do better than people who are unwilling to change."

Military initiative will require continuous victories. Since the guerrilla is usually weak at the outset . . . these may be only small successes, but such tactical self-sacrifice at the beginning may be necessary for eventual victory.

BARD E. O'NEILL, *THE ANALYSIS OF INSURGENCY*

CHAPTER NINE

THE CRITICAL 25 PERCENT: GIVING YOUR REQUEST A COMPETITIVE EDGE

[The guerrilla soldier] must be indefatigable. He must be able to produce another effort at the moment when weariness seems intolerable. Profound conviction, expressed in every line of his face, forces him to take another step, and this is not the last one, since it will be followed by another and another and another until he arrives at the place designated by his chiefs.

CHE GUEVARA, *GUERRILLA WARFARE*

When you have met with your grantmaker and submitted a proposal, you may be tempted to consider your work done. However, unless your award was decided upon before the proposal was prepared, you still have "miles to go before you sleep." This is not the time to sit back and indulge in the fantasy that your compelling document speaks for itself, or that your project will be awarded support on its merit alone.

The effort you must expend is certainly less now, but you should still plan to spend approximately 25 percent as much time, energy, and resources on postsubmission activities as you did before. This critical phase of the grantseeking process focuses on advocacy—persuading the grantmaker that your organization and your project are more deserving of support than those of others. Postsubmission activities are rarely if ever discussed in educational programs for nonprofit managers. That does not make them any less important; if anything, they are more important, as they often separate the winners from the losers.

As indicated in the last chapter, your grantmaker may offer an opportunity to improve your chances of success by inviting you to a postsubmission meeting at her office, or by making a site visit to your organization. If not, it's up to you to take the initiative.

Just as the outcome of a war can depend on the quiet, often secret activities of underground forces, the outcome of the grantseeking process is often determined by activities you pursue with utmost care and discretion after the proposal is submitted. The goal is to subtly influence the grantmaker's decision.

Getting the Lay of the Land

You scoped out the territory when you began your grantseeking activities, and now you must also do some reconnaissance to understand the basic contours of the landscape on which your advocacy campaign will be waged. This is a matter of learning about your grantmaker's decision-making process. Such information is rarely published, but grantmakers are almost always willing to share it if you ask. And you should ask, for two reasons. First, through a positive response you gain information that is critically important to you and to those who will become your advocates. Second, it impresses the grantmaker by indicating that you understand how the process works and that you intend to follow through after your proposal has been submitted. Here are the questions you should bring up:

- Who is involved in reviewing the proposal?
- What are the phases of the grantmaking process?
- What is the timetable?
- When will applicants who make the first cut be notified?
- Will a site visit be scheduled? If so, when?
- When and how will grantees be notified?

Once you understand these things, you can develop specific strategies for advocacy. An effective advocacy network is built in much the same as any other resource network.

Organizing Your Advocacy Campaign

Every project is unique and every campaign will vary in its details. But all advocacy campaigns require that you address the same six key questions:

- Whom should you recruit as your advocates?
- When should you recruit your advocates?
- What information do your advocates need?
- How can you motivate your advocates?
- What do you want your advocates to do for you?
- Where can you get help?

Whom Should You Recruit as Advocates?

In selecting advocates, consider these criteria:

- *Credibility.* If your grantmaker lacks confidence in what your advocate says, the advocate will not only do little good but may actually hurt your cause. So choose your associates with care: work with people of known credibility.
- *Connection.* Your advocate should be known to your grantmaker. Ideally, an advocate has an ongoing relationship with the grantmaker.
- *Knowledge.* Your advocate needs to know about you and about your project.

You may be wondering why an advocate can work more effectively on behalf of your project than you can. In essence, your grantmaker is more likely to believe and respond to an advocate because she knows him. Good advocates, like good members of an underground organization, tend to be "friendly natives"—insiders who are familiar with the terrain and who have local connections. They can get things done that are impossible for outsiders like you. These indigenous forces can advance your cause in ways that are simply not open to you.

Prospective advocates, for example, may include other program officers or executives with the same grantmaking organization. Or they may be program officers with another organization that collaborates with your grantmaker. Ideally, they know you well enough to speak eloquently and persuasively about you and your work, based on direct experience. In some cases, however, you may not be able to identify anyone who knows both you and your grantmaker; the best strategy then is to find someone who knows you and also knows a prospective advocate (someone who knows your grantmaker). You can then ask this intermediary to recruit the candidate on your behalf. This may seem circuitous, but asking people you know to recruit people they know is a basic networking strategy; in your advocacy campaign as in most other social and political activities, you must be able to network effectively.

Natural Advocates. The people who can speak most easily on your behalf are those closest to you and your project. These natural advocates may include colleagues who are collaborating on your project. Remember that just as people have their own friends, so do organizations. Do not hesitate to draw on any resources available to you.

If you are seeking a government grant, your natural advocates include the public officials who represent you at the city, county, state, or national level. As a voter, as a person who represents other constituents, and perhaps as a donor or volunteer, you have a right to expect your elected officials to go to bat for you. You can also seek the support of people who represent local, state, or regional organizations active in the same field as your grantmaking agency. For example:

- If you are seeking a federal grant to support an educational program, it makes sense to ask a representative of your state department of education to act as your advocate.
- If you are seeking a federal grant to support an economic development program, you could approach a representative of your local or state chamber of commerce.
- If you are seeking federal funds for a medical research project, you might ask a representative of your local or state department of health.

What About Clout? To design an effective advocacy campaign, it is essential to understand *clout*—power, influence, and control. In these matters, two realities must be kept in mind.

First, everyone's influence is limited, as influence is basically a zero-sum game. That is, an advocate who uses chits (units of influence) on your behalf will have less influence to use on behalf of someone or something else. Respect this reality. Before you ask someone to use a chit on behalf of your project, make sure that from your point of view it represents the best use of the limited resources available to that person.

Second, as the saying goes, "there ain't no such thing as a free lunch." Every time someone grants a favor, the person for whom the favor is done incurs an obligation. The payback may or may not involve exact reciprocity, such as a dollar-for-dollar contribution, but one way or another, chits must eventually be exchanged. So when you ask people to act as your advocates, keep in mind that you are asking them to incur obligations on your behalf. Down the line, be sure to reciprocate if an opportunity should present itself.

Who Has Clout? If you're not sure where to begin looking for influence, remember that clout usually has something to do with resources. As "Deep Throat," the secret Watergate source, told *Washington Post* reporters Robert Woodward and Carl Bernstein, "Follow the money!"

People who invest in a person or an organization become known as business friends. Different forms of investment capital are meaningful in different contexts:

- People who contribute significant dollars or direct significant numbers of votes to a winning candidate become business friends of the elected official. If you are trying to recruit a legislator to act as your advocate, then a major contributor to his or her campaign can probably open the door for you. If you are fortunate enough to have such a person on your board or among your friends, his involvement will, at the very least, assure you a receptive hearing.

- If you are pursuing a government grant, the legislators who serve on the appropriations or oversight committee for the agency may be able to influence the grantmaking process, despite any agency staffers' protestations to the contrary.

- If you are trying to influence decision makers at a foundation, neither cash nor votes will come into play. What counts in this case is the opinions of the foundation's trustees or those of the members of its advisory committee.

- If you are trying to secure a grant from a corporation or corporate foundation, the people who can help you are the company's senior executives or members of its board of directors.

Gorilla Grants. Identifying people with clout is largely a matter of common sense. But it is essential to be aware of the sensitivities involved in working the system this way. There is a definite potential downside; grantmaker staff members may feel coerced when such leverage is exerted, and this can interfere with the relationships you are trying to build with them. Grantmakers sometimes refer to grants awarded under such pressure as "gorilla grants" (as in the old joke, "What does a 500-pound gorilla eat for lunch? Anything he wants!")

When securing a specific grant is more important to you than long-term support from the grantmaker, however, it may make sense to risk alienating staff affections by recruiting a "gorilla" advocate. All else being equal, the influence of your advocate may be sufficient to win an award. For example, if you are seeking a grant from a corporate foundation and the company's board chairperson promotes your project, you will probably win an award so long as the project is sound and well presented. Likewise, if you are seeking a grant from a federal agency and the ranking majority member of its appropriations committee lobbies vigorously for your project, you will almost always win an award, so long as you have a good idea and describe it cogently in your proposal.

It may also be wise to recruit a "gorilla" advocate if you are confident that the person will be able to continue to help you in the future. For instance, if you are seeking a corporate grant and the chair of the corporate board also serves on the governing board of your organization, it probably makes sense to recruit him as an advocate. On the other hand, if your board member should find himself in a controversial position or at a tenuous juncture in his career, you might do better in the long run by working directly with the staff person, rather than risking disaffection by going over her head.

When Should You Recruit Your Advocates?

Just as agents in place are often recruited long before their services are needed, you should recruit prospective advocates for your organization as early as possible. Even if you are not currently seeking funds for a project, you almost certainly will in the future; if you wait until you *need* a favor, it may be too late to cultivate the kind of relationship that generates the best advocacy.

For this reason, provide information about your organization on a regular basis to a targeted group of influential people who may be able to help you in the future. Depending on the nature of your organization, such a group might include:

- Your state and federal legislators
- Officials of your local chamber of commerce
- Members of your local school board
- Members of your health care policymaking body
- Other public figures who may be interested in your work

When planning to seek funding for a project, you can alert the members of your "underground" network of advocates, just to give them a "heads up!" They can then begin listening at cocktail parties, talking up your organization on the golf course, and otherwise gathering and disseminating information on your behalf.

As your plans progress, keep the members of your underground informed. Let them know when you prepare and submit your proposal and what kind of feedback you get from the grantmaker. Take care, however, not to violate any expectations of confidentiality that your grantmaker expresses.

What Information Do Your Advocates Need?

To equip your advocates, prepare information about your project in a format they can easily use and that presents your message in a compelling fashion. Before meeting with a prospective advocate, share a copy of the full proposal you have submitted to the grantmaker. This will advance your cause in two ways: first, the person may actually be interested and review your proposal to become better informed, and second, a well-constructed, cogent document builds your credibility and helps pre-sell your case.

Keeping It Brief. Never assume, however, that your prospective advocate will actually read your proposal. Most people who would make effective advocates are very busy. If you have read books on proposal writing, you probably learned all about the virtues of brevity, clarity, and simplicity. Despite unanimous agreement on the desirability of these proposal traits, most grantseekers write proposals that contain more information than most prospective advocates need or want. Therefore, provide a very concise executive summary of your proposal (no longer than two pages) and a one-page financial summary, so all the key aspects of your budget can be seen at a glance. After sending these to the prospective advocate along with a copy of the full proposal, make an appointment to sit down with him and discuss your project.

For this meeting, prepare a personal briefing that summarizes your project and emphasizes how it can also benefit the prospective advocate. The best format for such a presentation is a short version of your story told in the form of headlines, with bullet points supporting each headline. If you feel compelled to provide more information, leave behind copies of your briefing notes.

Many other vehicles can be employed to communicate the merits of your project, and you should use as many as possible. For example, share copies of any recent articles about your organization that have appeared in local newspapers or magazines. The Institute for Government Public Information recently studied thirty different information sources to determine which ones members of Congress found most persuasive; articles in newspapers published in the legislators' home districts ranked highest.[1]

Next to local newspaper articles come telephone calls from constituents, personal letters, and electronic mail messages; all can help reinforce the importance of your project. Keep in mind, however, that your prospective advocates are very busy and that your project is only one of many that may interest them. To be heard above the din of competing messages, your communication must be in a format that overcomes or stands beyond the advocate's overstimulation. Make it easy to grasp all the salient points within seconds, rather than minutes. And make it clear what goals you have for the advocacy.

Communicating with Legislators. If you are pursuing a government grant and have decided to ask a particular legislator to be your advocate, you should understand and appreciate the volume of such requests that legislators receive. Respect the overloaded calendars and in-boxes they are all juggling. Washington-watchers report that every day, the average member of Congress receives hundreds if not thousands of pieces of mail, as well as hundreds of phone calls; in addition, a single day's calendar may include twenty to forty meetings. The exact numbers, of course, vary with the legislator's seniority, responsibilities, and personality. But clearly, the shorter your message and the easier it is to grasp, the more likely it will be heard.

Scheduled meetings with legislators are frequently preempted by a crucial vote, debate, or committee meeting. If this happens (and it does about 90 percent of the time), you will probably be invited to meet with one of the legislator's aides. In that case, proceed as planned. The aides do most of the legwork anyway, so you will be speaking with someone who is responsible for crafting the specifics of the legislator's positions on key issues.

How Can You Motivate Your Advocates?

In motivating advocates, the key is to make it clear how supporting your organization and project can benefit them too, or advance a cause in which they believe. The specifics, of course, depend on the individual.

Motivating the Elected Official. To every elected official who wants to stay in office, the most valuable commodity is votes. If your project has the potential to benefit voters directly, you can point out how its success will demonstrate the official's commitment to serving constituents.

One of the best ways for public officials to keep their constituents happy is to keep the local economy humming. Keeping current jobs and creating new ones is always paramount; if your project will help retain or create jobs (beyond your own), you can develop an economic impact forecast and share it with the legislator.

Remember, too, that campaign contributions are the lifeblood of any politician. Just as contributors can open doors, they can also influence a legislator to work on behalf of your project. An important point to keep in mind, however, is that yesterday's help is old news. Politicians, like anyone else, are eager to know not only what you have done for them lately but also what you plan to do for them in the immediate future. A prospective contributor actually occupies the most powerful position of all; tomorrow's contributions can be counted on to win a legislator's heart, as well as his attention.

Motivating the Corporate Executive. Although some contend that "corporate philanthropy" is an oxymoron, corporate foundations do provide approximately 5 percent of all private philanthropy. Their contributions amounted to some $6.1 billion in the United States in 1994, not including direct business-related contributions made through public affairs or advertising budgets.[2]

As noted earlier, people who work for corporate foundations walk a tightrope between Internal Revenue Service rules and shareholder responsibilities. On one hand, the IRS prohibits corporate foundations from making grants that directly enhance corporate profits. On the other, both shareholder responsibilities and good business practice dictate that corporate grants reflect some positive relationship to the bottom line. Therefore, if you want to recruit an advocate whose main interest is corporate well-being, concentrate on any potential your project may have for enhancing profits, either indirectly or in the long term.

It is not difficult, for example, to sell oil company executives on the merits of supporting fellowships for graduate students in geology. These are consistent with IRS guidelines, help build the business, and satisfy the expectations of stockholders by promoting research in a field of importance to the company even as they serve as a subtle and effective recruitment tool for prospective employees. This is the kind of approach that will attract the support of a corporate executive. Describe your project in a way that makes clear how the company will benefit, and you will have an enthusiastic advocate.

Motivating the Foundation Executive. Foundations, unlike corporations and government agencies, exist to fulfill a philanthropic mission, so the foundation executive must be approached from an altruistic point of view. Research the mission of the foundation and think about how your project can advance it. A foundation's mission may be as broad as improving health care in America (the Robert Wood Johnson Foundation) or as narrow as promoting the performance of Gregorian chants in Swiss monasteries (the Dom Mocquereau Foundation, recently disbanded).[3]

For community foundations the universal mission is to improve the quality of life in the community, but you are well advised to find out more. Most community foundations engage in strategic planning in order to set specific priorities; try to learn the current priorities, and consider how your project might help fulfill them.

In approaching foundation executives (or, for that matter, prospective advocates), emphasize that your project will advance the values that are most important to them and their organizations. At the same time, make the connection explicit enough so it becomes clear that your work will advance their specific agendas.

What Do You Want Your Advocate to Do?

Once your prospective advocate has agreed to help, his first question will be, "What can I do for you?" Ask him to make inquiries at the grantmaking organization and share with you any information that might help in planning your follow-through activities and in keeping your expectations realistic. None of this should be done in such a way or to such an extent that any moral or ethical constraints are violated. What you seek are insights that can help to frame your conversations with the grantmaker and that provide you with valuable perspective on your grantseeking activities.

In their contacts with the grantmaker, your advocates should emphasize how supporting your request meshes with the grantmaker's priorities and strategic stance. As we have indicated, grantmakers must often distribute funds according to geography or specific areas of interest. Learning about such patterns and priorities can help you target your advocacy efforts and keep your expectations at a realistic level.

In statewide grant programs, for example, funding must usually be distributed among regions, if not specific counties, within a state. If a large number of applications are received from a specific region, county, or city, the competition there will clearly be intense. On the other hand, if there is a paucity of applications from your part of the state, you will stand a better chance of winning an award.

Specific areas of interest may or may not be published in a grantmaker's request for proposals. If they are not, your advocate can probably elicit this information. You, in turn, can infer from it how interested the grantmaker might actually be in your project. If your project coincides with the grantmaker's highest priority, you know your project has a better than average chance of receiving support and you can give more attention to the effort. But if it doesn't, you know not to use up too many chits trying to win a grant and to concentrate on more promising opportunities.

Grantmakers often have unpublished agendas. Some may be interested in attracting new grantees to a program that has been in existence for some time; others may prefer to continue to support their current grantees. You have no control over such preferences, but knowing about them can help you manage your advocacy resources as effectively as possible. If your project meshes with the grantmaker's unpublished agenda, you can put on a full-court press; if it doesn't, any efforts will probably be in vain and you can save your resources.

Your advocate may be able to glean additional information that could be helpful in the interval between the submission of your proposal and the announcement of grant decisions. For instance, the grantmaker may volunteer information on which individuals are most influential in the decision-making process. In that event, you can make a special effort to see that the benefits of your project are explained to those individuals. Or your advocate may learn that a first cut has already been made and your proposal either made the cut or was eliminated; you can then adjust your expectations and follow-through activities accordingly.

Some of these things may seem to straddle the fence in terms of confidentiality. But let your advocates know that you do not expect them, while gathering intelligence, to cross any line that causes them discomfort. At the same time, of course, tell them you want to learn as much as possible about the grantmaker's priorities and challenges.

This is the crux of the issue: you want to enter into a collaborative venture with the grantmaker, and the success of the collaboration is determined by the quality of your relationship; the basis of this relationship is understanding your partner. If advocates can comfortably discover and share information that helps you better understand your grantmaker, they make a positive difference in your quest for support.

What specific action steps should an advocate take to encourage a grantmaker to see the value in your project? For many grantseekers, this is a challenging question. When it comes to managing volunteers, most nonprofit executives tend to be rather control-oriented, but here you need to loosen the reins. Deploying advocates requires a certain leap of faith.

Remember, your advocates know your grantmaker better than you do, or you wouldn't have recruited them. Therefore, trust to their discretion about how best to accomplish their missions. You must assume that, as "friendly natives," they understand the system better than you do—or at least well enough to be effective. This dynamic is actually another example of the "guerrilla" quality of grantseeking; there are no rules and very few guidelines for this kind of advocacy. Each interaction is highly individual and idiosyncratic. But so long as you have selected your advocates carefully and provided them with the appropriate information, you can rest assured that their influence will be positive.

Where Can You Get Help?

As in other aspects of the grantseeking process, all the activities we have just discussed may sound like a lot of work, and they certainly are. You may wonder if there is a way to get the job done more quickly and with less effort. The answer is yes or no, depending (as in so many other activities) on whether you have money. If you do, you can buy help.

In Chapter Two, we talked about locating a fundraising consultant to help with grantseeking. Retaining counsel can save you time and effort, and ensure that your own time and energy are invested as efficiently and effectively as possible.

If you are pursuing government grants, you can buy help from registered lobbyists or from consulting firms who specialize in government relations or public affairs. People who are registered to conduct lobbying activities on the federal level are listed in the *American Lobbyists Directory*.[4] A comprehensive listing of federal lobbyists and the organizations they represent is available in *Washington Representatives, 1995*.[5] If you are uncertain about the kinds of services provided by professionals who call themselves government relations consultants, it's all in the introduction to *Washington Representatives*.

Your public library may have similar registries for your state, like the *List of Legislative Agents* published by the Ohio Joint Committee on Agency Rule Review. Few cities seem to have any formal registration process for people who work to influence decisions on the municipal level; if you are seeking a grant from a municipal agency and want help, you might ask for referrals from executive directors of organizations that have received grants from the same agency. Take into account, however, that you are consulting people who are your actual or potential competitors, and listen to what they say with an appropriate filter.

Also in Chapter Two, we suggested that the best way to work with fundraising counsel is to operate in a collaborative fashion, because you, the grantseeker, must participate to develop relationships with grantmakers. In the same vein, legislators say that they would prefer to hear from constituents directly rather than from a lobbyist. At any rate, if you make the presentation yourself you can be sure that the information is presented in a way that is consistent with your organization's mission and plans.

A final caveat: there are exceptions to every rule, and a small number of instances where advocacy efforts are not only unnecessary, but positively unwise. In a small number of organizations and programs, any attempts to influence the decision-making process are prohibited. If your grantmaker's guidelines indicate that this is the case, you will have to play by the rules if you want to stay in the game, let alone win.

A successful guerrilla knows more than the hidden mountain terrain unmarked on the military maps. He knows as well the political, religious and racial prejudices of the inhabitants. He knows the taboos, the local beliefs and superstitions, the particular grievances of particular strata and regions. He also knows the political personalities, their friendships and rivalries, their weaknesses and strengths. And naturally he knows their language and patois.

CHARLES W. THAYER, *GUERRILLA*

THE GUERRILLA GRANTSEEKER: FOCUSED, DISCIPLINED, PERSISTENT

What is guerrilla warfare?

It is a type of warfare characterized by irregular forces fighting small-scale, limited actions, generally in conjunction with a larger political-military strategy, against orthodox military forces.

ROBERT B. ASPREY, *WAR IN THE SHADOWS: THE GUERRILLA IN HISTORY*

As a well-trained "guerrilla grantseeker," you are now a member of an elite group of professionals who understand the realities of the grantseeking process and have armed themselves with the knowledge and skills essential to winning grants. Before you take the field, you know the odds against you and that your power is inferior to that of the grantmakers you must win over to your cause.

Nevertheless, you are not pessimistic; rather, you adopt an attitude that is realistic and pragmatic. You realize that you are in this for the long haul, that you cannot pursue indiscriminately every opportunity that presents itself. Instead, you will marshal and conserve your resources, pick your spots carefully, and commit yourself only to those engagements you believe you can win, even knowing that you will not win all the time. You will use your instincts and your imagination as well as your intelligence. You will learn everything you can about the grantseeking terrain, the grantmakers who occupy it, and the way the game is played.

You will recruit and train allies and auxiliaries, and prepare carefully and thoroughly for every encounter with the grantmaker. When the encounter comes, you will try to be at your very best—attentive, responsive, light on your feet, and ready for anything. Ultimately, you will win the trust and confidence of grantmakers, make them allies, and help them see that *your* cause is *their* cause. In essence, you will succeed by building sound and enduring relationships.

All this requires focus, discipline, and persistence. Grantseeking, like guerrilla warfare, is not for the faint of heart or those who want a "quick fix." There will be many days when your plans do not work, when the road you are traveling seems impossibly long, when your best efforts go unrewarded. By turns, you will feel confused, embarrassed, and exhausted.

But like other challenges, if these experiences don't kill you or drive you out of the business, they will make you a better and stronger person, professional, and grantseeker. You will learn not to waste your efforts on unpromising situations, to stay focused on your goal, and to keep moving forward with confidence in the ultimate outcome.

As a veteran of the grantseeking wars, I assure you that if you adhere faithfully to the principles outlined in this book, you will distinguish yourself as one of the select few who consistently emerge winners. Over the long haul, the results will justify your efforts; you will win grants that make it possible for your organization to advance, to enhance the lives of the people you serve, and to make your community and the world a better place.

I wish you success.

This is the basis, the essence of guerrilla fighting. Miraculously, a small band of men, the armed vanguard of the great popular force that supports them, goes on decisively to achieve an ideal, to establish a new society, to break the old molds of the outdated, and to achieve, finally, the social justice for which they fight.

CHE GUEVARA, *GUERRILLA WARFARE*

THE FOUNDATION CENTER DIRECTORY OF FREE FUNDING INFORMATION CENTERS

The Foundation Center is an independent national service organization established by foundations to provide an authoritative source of information on foundation and corporate giving. The New York, Washington, D.C., Atlanta, Cleveland, and San Francisco reference collections operated by the Foundation Center offer a wide variety of services and comprehensive collections of information on foundations and grants. Cooperating Collections are libraries, community foundations, and other nonprofit agencies that provide a core collection of Foundation Center publications and a variety of supplementary materials and services in areas useful to grantseekers. The core collection consists of:

The Foundation Directory 1 and 2, and Supplement

The Foundation 1000

Foundation Fundamentals

Foundation Giving

The Foundation Grants Index

The Foundation Grants Index Quarterly

Foundation Grants to Individuals

Guide to U.S. Foundations, Their Trustees, Officers, and Donors

The Foundation Center's Guide to Proposal Writing

The Literature of the Nonprofit Sector

National Directory of Corporate Giving

National Directory of Grantmaking Public Charities

National Guide to Funding in. . . . (Series)

Many of the network members make available for public use sets of private foundation information returns (IRS Form 990-PF) for their state and/or neighboring states. A complete set of U.S. foundation returns can be found at the New York and Washington, D.C., offices of the Foundation Center. The Atlanta, Cleveland, and San Francisco offices contain IRS Form 990-PF returns for the southeastern, midwestern, and western states, respectively. Those Cooperating Collections marked with a bullet (•) have sets of private foundation information returns for their state and/or neighboring states.

Because the collections vary in their hours, materials, and services, *it is recommended that you call the collection in advance.* To check on new locations or current information, call toll-free 1–800–424–9836, or visit our Web site at http://fdncenter.org/library/library.html.

Reference Collections Operated by the Foundation Center

The Foundation Center
8th Floor
79 Fifth Avenue
New York, NY 10003
(212) 620–4230

The Foundation Center
312 Sutter St., Rm. 312
San Francisco, CA 94108
(415) 397–0902

The Foundation Center
1001 Connecticut Ave., NW
Washington, DC 20036
(202) 331–1400

The Foundation Center
Kent H. Smith Library
1422 Euclid, Suite 1356
Cleveland, OH 44115
(216) 861–1933

The Foundation Center
Suite 150, Grand Lobby
Hurt Bldg., 50 Hurt Plaza
Atlanta, GA 30303
(404) 880–0094

Foundation Center Cooperating Collections

Alabama

- Birmingham Public Library
  Government Documents
  2100 Park Place
  Birmingham 35203
  (205) 226–3600

  Huntsville Public Library
  915 Monroe St.
  Huntsville 35801
  (205) 532–5940

- University of South Alabama
  Library Building
  Mobile 36688
  (334) 460–7025

- Auburn University at Montgomery
  Library
  7300 University Drive
  Montgomery 36117–3596
  (334) 244–3653

Alaska

- University of Alaska at Anchorage
  Library
  3211 Providence Drive
  Anchorage 99508
  (907) 786–1847

- Juneau Public Library
  Reference
  292 Marine Way
  Juneau 99801
  (907) 586–5267

Arizona

- Phoenix Public Library
  Business & Sciences Unit
  12 E. McDowell Rd.
  Phoenix 85004
  (602) 262–4636

- Tucson Pima Library
  101 N. Stone Ave.
  Tucson 87501
  (520) 791–4010

Arkansas

- Westark Community College—
  Borham Library
  5210 Grand Avenue
  Ft. Smith 72913
  (501) 788–7200

- Central Arkansas Library System
  700 Louisiana
  Little Rock 72201
  (501) 370–5952

  Pine Bluff-Jefferson County Library
  System
  200 E. Eighth
  Pine Bluff 71601
  (501) 534–2159

California

- Humboldt Area Foundation
  P.O. Box 99
  Bayside 95524
  (707) 442–2993

- Ventura County Community
  Foundation
  Funding and Information Resource
  Center
  1355 Del Norte Rd.
  Camarillo 93010
  (805) 988–0196

- California Community Foundation
  Funding Information Center
  606 S. Olive St., Suite 2400
  Los Angeles 90014–1526
  (213) 413–4042

- Oakland Nonprofit Resource Center
  1203 Preservation Pkwy., Suite 100
  Oakland 94612
  (510) 834–1010

- Grant & Resource Center of
  Northern California
  Building C, Suite A
  2280 Benton Dr.
  Redding 96003
  (916) 244–1219

  Los Angeles Public Library
  West Valley Regional Branch Library
  19036 Van Owen St.
  Reseda 91335
  (818) 345–4393

  Riverside City & County Public
  Library
  3021 Franklin Ave.
  Riverside 92502
  (714) 782–5201

Nonprofit Resource Center
Sacramento Public Library
828 I Street, 2nd Floor
Sacramento 95814
(916) 264–2772

- San Diego Community Foundation
  Funding Information Center
  101 West Broadway, Suite 1120
  San Diego 92101
  (619) 239–8815

  Nonprofit Development Center
  Library
  1922 The Alameda, Suite 212
  San Jose 95126
  (408) 248–9505

- Peninsula Community Foundation
  Funding Information Library
  1700 S. El Camino Real, R301
  San Mateo 94402–3049
  (415) 358–9392

  Los Angeles Public Library
  San Pedro Regional Branch
  9131 S. Gaffey St.
  San Pedro 90731
  (310) 548–7779

  Volunteer Center of Greater Orange
  County
  Nonprofit Management Assistance
  Center
  1901 E. 4th St., Ste. 100
  Santa Ana 92705
  (714) 953–1655

  Santa Barbara Public Library
  40 E. Anapamu St.
  Santa Barbara 93101
  (805) 962–7653

Santa Monica Public Library
1343 Sixth St.
Santa Monica 90401–1603
(310) 458–8600

Sonoma County Library
3rd & E Streets
Santa Rosa 95404
(707) 545–0831

Seaside Branch Library
550 Harcourt St.
Seaside 93955
(408) 899–8131

Colorado

El Pomar Nonprofit Resource
   Center
1661 Mesa Ave.
Colorado Springs 80906
(800) 554–7711

- Denver Public Library
  General Reference
  10 West 14th Ave. Pkwy.
  Denver 80204
  (303) 640–6200

Connecticut

Danbury Public Library
170 Main St.
Danbury 06810
(203) 797–4527

- Greenwich Library
  101 West Putnam Ave.
  Greenwich 06830
  (203) 622–7910

- Hartford Public Library
  500 Main St.
  Hartford 06103
  (203) 293–6000

D.A.T.A.
70 Audubon St.
New Haven 06510
(203) 772–1345

Delaware

- University of Delaware
  Hugh Morris Library
  Newark 19717–5267
  (302) 831–2432

Florida

Volusia County Library Center
City Island
Daytona Beach 32014–4484
(904) 257–6036

- Nova Southeastern University
  Einstein Library
  3301 College Ave.
  Fort Lauderdale 33314
  (305) 475–7050

Indian River Community College
Charles S. Miley Learning Resource
  Center
3209 Virginia Ave.
Fort Pierce 34981–5599
(407) 462–4757

• Jacksonville Public Libraries
  Grants Resource Center
  122 N. Ocean St.
  Jacksonville 32202
  (904) 630–2665

• Miami-Dade Public Library
  Humanities/Social Science
  101 W. Flagler St.
  Miami 33130
  (305) 375–5575

• Orlando Public Library
  Social Sciences Department
  101 E. Central Blvd.
  Orlando 32801
  (407) 425–4694

Selby Public Library
Reference
1001 Blvd. of the Arts
Sarasota 34236
(941) 951–5501

• Tampa-Hillsborough County Public
  Library
  900 N. Ashley Drive
  Tampa 33602
  (813) 273–3628

• Community Foundation of Palm
  Beach & Martin Counties
  324 Datura St., Suite 340
  West Palm Beach 33401
  (407) 659–6800

Georgia

• Atlanta-Fulton Public Library
  Foundation Collection—Ivan Allen
    Department
  1 Margaret Mitchell Square
  Atlanta 30303–1089
  (404) 730–1900

• Thomas County Public Library
  201 N. Madison St.
  Thomasville 31792
  (912) 225–5252

Hawaii

• University of Hawaii
  Hamilton Library
  2550 The Mall
  Honolulu 96822
  (808) 956–7214

Hawaii Community Foundation
  Resource Library
900 Fort St., Suite 1300
Honolulu 96813
(808) 537–6333

Idaho

- Boise Public Library
  715 S. Capitol Blvd.
  Boise 83702
  (208) 384–4024

- Caldwell Public Library
  1010 Dearborn St.
  Caldwell 83605
  (208) 459–3242

Illinois

- Donors Forum of Chicago
  53 W. Jackson Blvd., Suite 430
  Chicago 60604–3608
  (312) 431–0265

  Rock Island Public Library
  401 19th St.
  Rock Island 61201
  (309) 788–7627

- Evanston Public Library
  1703 Orrington Ave.
  Evanston 60201
  (708) 866–0305

- University of Illinois at Springfield
  Brookens Library
  Shepherd Road
  Springfield 62794–9243
  (217) 786–6633

Indiana

- Allen County Public Library
  900 Webster St.
  Ft. Wayne 46802
  (219) 424–0544

  Indiana University of Northwest
    Library
  3400 Broadway
  Gary 46408
  (219) 980–6582

- Indianapolis-Marion County Public
    Library
  Social Sciences
  40 E. St. Clair
  Indianapolis 46206
  (317) 269–1733

Iowa

- Cedar Rapids Public Library
  Foundation Center Collection
  500 First St., SE
  Cedar Rapids 52401
  (319) 398–5123

- Southwestern Community College
  Learning Resource Center
  1501 W. Townline Rd.
  Creston 50801
  (515) 782–7081

- Public Library of Des Moines
  100 Locust
  Des Moines 50309–1791
  (515) 283–4152

- Sioux City Public Library
  529 Pierce St.
  Sioux City 51101–1202
  (712) 252–5669

Kansas

- Dodge City Public Library
  1001 2nd Ave.
  Dodge City 67801
  (316) 225–0248

- Wichita Public Library
  223 S. Main St.
  Wichita 67202
  (316) 262–0611

- Topeka and Shawnee County Public
    Library
  1515 SW 10th Ave.
  Topeka 66604–1374
  (913) 233–2040

Kentucky

- Western Kentucky University
  Helm-Cravens Library
  Bowling Green 42101–3576
  (502) 745–6125

- Lexington Public Library
  140 E. Main St.
  Lexington 40507–1376
  (606) 231–5520

- Louisville Free Public Library
  301 York Street
  Louisville 40203
  (502) 574–1611

Louisiana

- East Baton Rouge Parish Library
  Centroplex Branch Grants Collection
  120 St. Louis
  Baton Rouge 70802
  (504) 389–4960

- Beauregard Parish Library
  205 S. Washington Ave.
  De Ridder 70634
  (318) 463–6217

- New Orleans Public Library
  Business & Science Division
  219 Loyola Ave.
  New Orleans 70140
  (504) 596–2580

- Shreve Memorial Library
  424 Texas St.
  Shreveport 71120–1523
  (318) 226–5894

Maine

- Maine Grants Information Center
  University of Southern Maine
  P.O. Box 9301, 314 Forrest Ave.
  Portland 04104–9301
  (207) 780–4411

Maryland

- Enoch Pratt Free Library
  Social Science & History
  400 Cathedral St.
  Baltimore 21201
  (410) 396–5430

Massachusetts

- Associated Grantmakers of
    Massachusetts
  294 Washington St., Suite 840
  Boston 02108
  (617) 426–2606

- Boston Public Library
  Soc. Sci. Reference
  666 Boylston St.
  Boston 02117
  (617) 536–5400

Western Massachusetts Funding
    Resource Center
65 Elliot St.
Springfield 01101–1730
(413) 732–3175

- Worcester Public Library
  Grants Resource Center
  Salem Square
  Worcester 01608
  (508) 799–1655

Michigan

- Alpena County Library
  211 N. First St.
  Alpena 49707
  (517) 356–6188

- University of Michigan-Ann Arbor
  Graduate Library
  Reference & Research Services
      Department
  Ann Arbor 48109–1205
  (313) 764–9373

- Henry Ford Centennial Library
  Adult Services
  16301 Michigan Ave.
  Dearborn 48126
  (313) 943–2330

- Willard Public Library
  7 W. Van Buren St.
  Battle Creek 49017
  (616) 968–8166

- Wayne State University
  Purdy/Kresge Library
  5265 Cass Avenue
  Detroit 48202
  (313) 577–6424

- Michigan State University Libraries
  Social Sciences/Humanities
  Main Library
  East Lansing 48824–1048
  (517) 353–8818

- Farmington Community Library
  32737 West 12 Mile Rd.
  Farmington Hills 48018
  (810) 553–0300

- University of Michigan—Flint
  Library
  Flint 48502–2186
  (810) 762–3408

- Grand Rapids Public Library
  Business Dept.—3rd Floor
  60 Library Plaza NE
  Grand Rapids 49503–3093
  (616) 456–3600

  Michigan Technological University
  Van Pelt Library
  1400 Townsend Dr.
  Houghton 49931
  (906) 487–2507

Maud Preston Palenske Memorial
  Library
500 Market St.
Saint Joseph 49085
(616) 983–7167

Sault Ste. Marie Area Public Schools
Office of Compensatory Education
460 W. Spruce St.
Sault Ste. Marie 49783–1874
(906) 635–6618

- Northwestern Michigan College
  Mark & Helen Osterin Library
  1701 E. Front St.
  Traverse City 49684
  (616) 922–1060

Minnesota

- Duluth Public Library
  520 W. Superior St.
  Duluth 55802
  (218) 723–3802

- Southwest State University
  University Library
  Marshall 56258
  (507) 537–6176

  St. Paul Public Library
  90 W. Fourth St.
  St. Paul 55102
  (612) 292–6307

Rochester Public Library
101 2nd St. SE
Rochester 55904–3776
(507) 285–8002

- Minneapolis Public Library
  Sociology Department
  300 Nicollet Mall
  Minneapolis 55401
  (612) 372–6555

Mississippi

- Jackson/Hinds Library System
  300 N. State St.
  Jackson 39201
  (601) 968–5803

Missouri

- Clearinghouse for Midcontinent
  Foundations
  University of Missouri
  5110 Cherry, Suite 310
  Kansas City 64110
  (816) 235–1176

- Kansas City Public Library
  311 E. 12th St.
  Kansas City 64106
  (816) 221–9650

- Metropolitan Association for
  Philanthropy, Inc.
  5615 Pershing Avenue, Suite 20
  St. Louis 63112
  (314) 361–3900

- Springfield-Greene County Library
  397 E. Central
  Springfield 65802
  (417) 837–5000

Montana

- Montana State University—Billings
  Library—Special Collections
  1500 North 30th St.
  Billings 59101–0298
  (406) 657–1662

- Bozeman Public Library
  220 E. Lamme
  Bozeman 59715
  (406) 582–2402

- Montana State Library
  Library Services
  1515 E. 6th Ave.
  Helena 59620
  (406) 444–3004

- University of Montana
  Maureen & Mike Mansfield Library
  Missoula 59812–1195
  (406) 243–6800

Nebraska

- University of Nebraska—Lincoln
  Love Library
  14th & R Streets
  Lincoln 68588–0410
  (402) 472–2848

- W. Dale Clark Library
  Social Sciences Department
  215 S. 15th St.
  Omaha 68102
  (402) 444–4826

Nevada

- Las Vegas-Clark County Library
  District
  1401 E. Flamingo
  Las Vegas 89119
  (702) 733–3642

- Washoe County Library
  301 S. Center St.
  Reno 89501
  (702) 785–4010

New Hampshire

- New Hampshire Charitable Fdn.
  37 Pleasant St.
  Concord 03301–4005
  (603) 225–6641

- Plymouth State College
  Herbert H. Lamson Library
  Plymouth 03264
  (603) 535–2258

New Jersey

- Cumberland County Library
  New Jersey Room
  800 E. Commerce St.
  Bridgeton 08302
  (609) 453–2210

- New Jersey State Library
  Governmental Reference Services
  185 W. State St.
  Trenton 08625–0520
  (609) 292–6220

- County College of Morris
  Learning Resource Center
  214 Center Grove Rd.
  Randolph 07869
  (201) 328–5296

- Free Public Library of Elizabeth
  11 S. Broad St.
  Elizabeth 07202
  (908) 354–6060

New Mexico

- Albuquerque Community
    Foundation
  3301 Menual NE, Ste. 30
  Albuquerque 87176–6960
  (505) 883–6240

- New Mexico State Library
  Information Services
  325 Don Gaspar
  Santa Fe 87501–2777
  (505) 827–3824

New York

- New York State Library
  Humanities Reference
  Cultural Education Center
  Empire State Plaza
  Albany 12230
  (518) 474–5355

  Suffolk Cooperative Library System
  627 N. Sunrise Service Rd.
  Bellport 11713
  (516) 286–1600

  Brooklyn Public Library
  Social Sciences Division
  Grand Army Plaza
  Brooklyn 11238
  (718) 780–7700

  Brooklyn in Touch Information
    Center, Inc.
  One Hanson Place—Room 2504
  Brooklyn 11243
  (718) 230–3200

New York Public Library
Bronx Reference Center
Fordham Branch
2556 Bainbridge Ave.
Bronx 10458
(718) 220–6575

- Plattsburgh Public Library
  19 Oak St.
  Plattsburgh 12901
  (518) 563–0921

Huntington Public Library
338 Main St.
Huntington 11743
(516) 427–5165

Queens Borough Public Library
Social Sciences Division
89–11 Merrick Blvd.
Jamaica 11432
(718) 990–0761

- Levittown Public Library
  1 Bluegrass Lane
  Levittown 11756
  (516) 731–5728

New York Public Library
Countee Cullen Branch Library
104 W. 136th St.
New York 10030
(212) 491–2070

- Buffalo & Erie County Public
  Library
  Business & Labor Dept.
  Lafayette Square
  Buffalo 14203
  (716) 858–7097

Adriance Memorial Library
Special Services Department
93 Market St.
Poughkeepsie 12601
(914) 485–3445

- Rochester Public Library
  Business, Economics & Law
  115 South Ave.
  Rochester 14604
  (716) 428–7328

Onondaga County Public Library
447 S. Salina St.
Syracuse 13202–2494
(315) 435–1800

Utica Public Library
303 Genesee St.
Utica 13501
(315) 735–2279

White Plains Public Library
100 Martine Ave.
White Plains 10601
(914) 422–1480

North Carolina

- Community Fdn. of Western North
  Carolina
  Learning Resources Center
  14 College St.
  P.O. Box 1888
  Asheville 28801
  (704) 254–4960

- State Library of North Carolina
  Government and Business Services
  Archives Bldg., 109 E. Jones St.
  Raleigh 27601
  (919) 733–3270

- The Duke Endowment
  100 N. Tryon St., Suite 3500
  Charlotte 28202
  (704) 376–0291

  Durham County Public Library
  301 North Roxboro
  Durham 27702
  (919) 560–0110

- Forsyth County Public Library
  660 W. 5th St.
  Winston-Salem 27101
  (910) 727–2680

North Dakota

- Bismarck Public Library
  515 N. Fifth St.
  Bismarck 58501
  (701) 222–6410

- Fargo Public Library
  102 N. 3rd St.
  Fargo 58102
  (701) 241–1491

Ohio

  Stark County District Library
  Humanities
  715 Market Ave. N.
  Canton 44702
  (216) 452–0665

- Public Library of Cincinnati &
  Hamilton County
  Grants Resource Center
  800 Vine St.—Library Square
  Cincinnati 45202–2071
  (513) 369–6940

- Dayton & Montgomery County
  Public Library
  Grants Resource Center
  215 E. Third St.
  Dayton 45402
  (513) 227–9500 x211

  Muskingum County Library
  220 N. 5th St.
  Zanesville 43701
  (614) 453–0391

- Mansfield/Richland County Public
  Library
  42 W. 3rd St.
  Mansfield 44902
  (419) 521–3110

- Toledo-Lucas County Public Library
  Social Sciences Department
  325 Michigan St.
  Toledo 43624–1614
  (419) 259–5245

- Public Library of Youngstown &
  Mahoning County
  305 Wick Ave.
  Youngstown 44503
  (216) 744–8636

  Columbus Metropolitan Library
  Business and Technology
  96 S. Grant Ave.
  Columbus 43215
  (614) 645–2590

Oklahoma

- Oklahoma City University
  Dulaney Browne Library
  2501 N. Blackwelder
  Oklahoma City 73106
  (405) 521–5072

- Tulsa City-County Library
  400 Civic Center
  Tulsa 74103
  (918) 596–7944

Oregon

Oregon Institute of Technology
  Library
3201 Campus Dr.
Klamath Falls 97601–8801
(503) 885–1773

- Pacific Non-Profit Network
  Grantsmanship Resource Library
  33 N. Central, Suite 211
  Medford 97501
  (503) 779–6044

Multnomah County Library
Government Documents
801 SW Tenth Ave.
Portland 97205
(503) 248–5123

- Oregon State Library
  State Library Building
  Salem 97310
  (503) 378–4277

Pennsylvania

Northampton Community College
Learning Resources Center
3835 Green Pond Rd.
Bethlehem 18017
(610) 861–5360

- Carnegie Library of Pittsburgh
  Foundation Collection
  4400 Forbes Ave.
  Pittsburgh 15213–4080
  (412) 622–1917

Pocono Northeast Development Fund
James Pettinger Memorial Library
1151 Oak St.
Pittston 18640–3795
(717) 655–5581

Erie County Library System
27 S. Park Row
Erie 16501
(814) 451–6927

Dauphin County Library System
Central Library
101 Walnut St.
Harrisburg 17101
(717) 234–4976

Lancaster County Public Library
125 N. Duke St.
Lancaster 17602
(717) 394–2651

Reading Public Library
100 South Fifth St.
Reading 19602
(610) 655–6355

- Martin Library
  159 Market St.
  York 17401
  (717) 846–5300

- Free Library of Philadelphia
  Regional Foundation Center
  Logan Square
  Philadelphia 19103
  (215) 686–5423

Rhode Island

- Providence Public Library
  225 Washington St.
  Providence 02906
  (401) 455–8088

South Carolina

- Anderson County Library
  202 East Greenville St.
  Anderson 29621
  (803) 260–4500

- Charleston County Library
  404 King St.
  Charleston 29403
  (803) 723–1645

- South Carolina State Library
  1500 Senate St.
  Columbia 29211
  (803) 734–8666

South Dakota

- South Dakota State Library
  800 Governors Drive
  Pierre 57501–2294
  (605) 773–5070
  (800) 592–1841 (SD residents)

- Siouxland Libraries
  201 N. Main Ave.
  Sioux Falls 57102–1132
  (605) 367–7081

Nonprofit Grants Assistance Center
Dakota State University
Business and Education Institute
3534 Southwestern Ave.
Sioux Falls 57105
(605) 367–5380

Tennessee

- Knox County Public Library
  500 W. Church Ave.
  Knoxville 37902
  (615) 544–5700

- Memphis & Shelby County Public
    Library
  1850 Peabody Ave.
  Memphis 38104
  (901) 725–8877

- Nashville Public Library
  Business Information Division
  225 Polk Ave.
  Nashville 37203
  (615) 862–5843

Texas

- Abilene Center for Nonprofit
    Management
  Funding Information Library
  500 N. Chestnut, Suite 1511
  Abilene 79604
  (915) 677–8166

- Amarillo Area Foundation
  700 First National Place
  801 S. Fillmore
  Amarillo 79101
  (806) 376–4521

- Hogg Foundation for Mental Health
  3001 Lake Austin Blvd.
  Austin 78703
  (512) 471–5041

- Dallas Public Library
  Urban Information
  1515 Young St.
  Dallas 75201
  (214) 670–1487

- El Paso Community Foundation
  201 E. Main St., Suite 1616
  El Paso 79901
  (915) 533–4020

- Texas A&M University at Corpus
    Christi
  Bell Library
  Reference Dept.
  6300 Ocean Dr.
  Corpus Christi 78412
  (512) 994–2608

- Houston Public Library
  Bibliographic Information Center
  500 McKinney
  Houston 77002
  (713) 236–1313

- Longview Public Library
  222 W. Cotton St.
  Longview 75601
  (903) 237–1352

- Lubbock Area Foundation, Inc.
  1655 Main St., Suite 209
  Lubbock 79401
  (806) 762–8061

- Funding Information Center
  530 McCullough, Suite 600
  San Antonio 78212–8270
  (210) 227–4333

Waco-McClennan County Library
1717 Austin Ave.
Waco 76701
(817) 750–5941

• North Texas Center for Nonprofit
  Management
624 Indiana, Suite 307
Wichita Falls 76301
(817) 322–4961

• Funding Information Center of Fort
  Worth
Texas Christian University Library
2800 S. University Dr.
Ft. Worth 76129
(817) 921–7664

Utah

Salt Lake City Public Library
209 East 500 South
Salt Lake City 84111
(801) 524–8200

Vermont

• Vermont Dept. of Libraries
Reference & Law Info. Services
109 State St.
Montpelier 05609
(802) 828–3268

Virginia

Hampton Public Library
4207 Victoria Blvd.
Hampton 23669
(804) 727–1312

• Richmond Public Library
Business, Science & Technology
101 East Franklin St.
Richmond 23219
(804) 780–8223

• Roanoke City Public Library System
Central Library
706 S. Jefferson St.
Roanoke 24016
(703) 981–2477

Washington

- Mid-Columbia Library
  405 South Dayton
  Kennewick 99336
  (509) 586–3156

- Seattle Public Library
  Science, Social Science
  1000 Fourth Ave.
  Seattle 98104
  (206) 386–4620

- Spokane Public Library
  Funding Information Center
  West 811 Main Ave.
  Spokane 99201
  (509) 626–5347

- United Way of Pierce County
  Center for Nonprofit Development
  1501 Pacific Ave., Suite 400
  P.O. Box 2215
  Tacoma 98401
  (206) 272–4263

  Greater Wenatchee Community
  Foundation at the Wenatchee
  Public Library
  310 Douglas St.
  Wenatchee 98807
  (509) 662–5021

West Virginia

- Kanawha County Public Library
  123 Capitol St.
  Charleston 25301
  (304) 343–4646

Wisconsin

- University of Wisconsin-Madison
  Memorial Library
  728 State St.
  Madison 53706
  (608) 262–3242

- University of Wisconsin—Stevens
  Point
  Library—Foundation Collection
  99 Reserve St.
  Stevens Point 54481–3897
  (715) 346–4204

- Marquette University Memorial
  Library
  Funding Information Center
  1415 W. Wisconsin Ave.
  Milwaukee 53201–3141
  (414) 288–1515

Wyoming

- Natrona County Public Library
  307 E. 2nd St.
  Casper 82601–2598
  (307) 237–4935

- Teton County Library
  320 S. King St.
  Jackson 83001
  (307) 733–2164

  Rock Springs Library
  400 C St.
  Rock Springs 82901
  (307) 352–6667

- Laramie County Community
    College
  Instructional Resource Center
  1400 E. College Dr.
  Cheyenne 82007–3299
  (307) 778–1206

- Campbell County Public Library
  2101 4-J Road
  Gillette 82716
  (307) 682–3223

Puerto Rico

University of Puerto Rico
Ponce Technological College Library
Box 7186
Ponce 00732
(809) 844–8181

Universidad del Sagrado Corazon
M.M.T. Guevara Library
Santurce 00914
(809) 728–1515 x 4357

Participants in the Foundation Center's Cooperating Collections network are libraries or nonprofit information centers that provide fundraising information and other funding-related technical assistance in their communities. Cooperating Collections agree to provide free public access to a basic collection of Foundation Center publications during a regular schedule of hours, offering free funding research guidance to all visitors. Many also provide a variety of services for local nonprofit organizations, using staff or volunteers to prepare special materials, organize workshops, or conduct orientations.

The Foundation Center welcomes inquiries from libraries or information centers in the U.S. interested in providing this type of public information service. If you are interested in establishing a funding information library for the use of nonprofit organizations in your area or in learning more about the program, please write to: Judith Margolin, Vice President for Public Services, The Foundation Center, 79 Fifth Avenue, New York, NY 10003–3076.

BUDGET PREPARATION GUIDELINES

EXHIBIT B.1. PROJECT BUDGET PREPARATION GUIDELINES.

OVERVIEW

Two important components of your grant application are a line-item budget and budget narrative. Please follow the guidelines below carefully.

LINE-ITEM BUDGET

- The line-item budget form should include revenues and expenses associated with the proposed project.

- Revenues should be categorized as <u>committed</u> or <u>anticipated</u>.

- For multi-year requests, grantseekers should complete a separate budget form for each full or partial year of requested funding as well as the budget summary sheets.

- Please note that in-kind contributions should be shown and made part of the narrative, but **should not be included** in the total projected revenues line.

- Please **type** all information on the forms.

- Each budget form should include the name of a contact person familiar with the project budget.

BUDGET NARRATIVE

- The budget narrative should include an explanation of every line item for which you are requesting Foundation support. For example:

    Project Director: This position is accountable for planning, organizing and directing the implementation and operations of the project. Specific responsibilities include directing staff, orientation, training and evaluation in accordance with department standards. The project director also directly supervises three case managers.

    Postage: The total requested postage budget is $2,500. This includes mailing routine correspondence as well as the community health assessment questionnaire. The questionnaire is an integral component of our activities in year one as outlined on page 22 of our proposal. The total number of questionnaires to be mailed is 7,500 at a cost of $2,175. The $325 balance is for the mailing of routine correspondence.

- The fringe benefits line-item should list which benefits have been included, e.g. FICA, pension, worker's compensation.

- Describe the basis for calculation of any direct costs, including any budget items which are part of your indirect cost.

EXHIBIT B2. THE CLEVELAND FOUNDATION BUDGET SUMMARY.

Requesting Organization: _____

Project Title: _____

SUMMARY OF PROJECT REVENUES

Revenues (committed and anticipated)	Year 1	Year 2	Year 3	Total Project Revenues
Grants and other support				
Government	$_____	$_____	$_____	$_____
Foundations and Corporations				
The Cleveland Foundation	$_____	$_____	$_____	$_____
_____	$_____	$_____	$_____	$_____
_____	$_____	$_____	$_____	$_____
_____	$_____	$_____	$_____	$_____
_____	$_____	$_____	$_____	$_____
Organizational Income	$_____	$_____	$_____	$_____
Other	$_____	$_____	$_____	$_____
Total Project Revenues	$_____	$_____	$_____	$_____
In-Kind (not included in total)	$_____	$_____	$_____	$_____

SUMMARY OF PROJECT EXPENSES

Expenses	Year 1	Year 2	Year 3	Total Project Expenses
Personnel Expenses				
Staff Costs	$_____	$_____	$_____	$_____
Fringes	$_____	$_____	$_____	$_____
Personnel Expenses Subtotal	$_____	$_____	$_____	$_____
Non-Personnel Expenses				
Contract Services	$_____	$_____	$_____	$_____
Office Space	$_____	$_____	$_____	$_____
Equipment/Supplies	$_____	$_____	$_____	$_____
Travel/Related Expenses	$_____	$_____	$_____	$_____
Other	$_____	$_____	$_____	$_____
Non-Personnel Expenses Subtotal	$_____	$_____	$_____	$_____
Total Project Expenses	$_____	$_____	$_____	$_____

EXHIBIT B3. THE CLEVELAND FOUNDATION PROJECT BUDGET REQUEST.

(Please copy form for multiple-year projects)

Requesting Organization: _____

Project Title: _____

Project Duration: From _____ To _____

Total amount requested from The Cleveland Foundation: $ _____

PROJECT REVENUES

Grants and other support

Government	Committed	Anticipated	Total
City	$_____	$_____	$_____
County	$_____	$_____	$_____
State	$_____	$_____	$_____
Federal	$_____	$_____	$_____
Government Subtotal	$_____	$_____	$_____

Foundations and Corporations (list separately)

	Committed	Anticipated	Total
The Cleveland Foundation	$_____	$_____	$_____
_____	$_____	$_____	$_____
_____	$_____	$_____	$_____
	$_____	$_____	$_____
Foundations and Corporations Subtotal	$_____	$_____	$_____

Organizational Income

	Committed	Anticipated	Total
Membership fees/dues	$_____	$_____	$_____
Contract services	$_____	$_____	$_____
Fundraising events	$_____	$_____	$_____
Other	$_____	$_____	$_____
Organizational Income Subtotal	$_____	$_____	$_____

Other (specify)

	Committed	Anticipated	Total
_____	$_____	$_____	$_____
_____	$_____	$_____	$_____
Other Subtotal	$_____	$_____	$_____
TOTAL PROJECT REVENUES	$_____	$_____	$_____

In-Kind (List below: *do not* include in total)

	Committed	Anticipated	Total
_____	$_____	$_____	$_____
_____	$_____	$_____	$_____
_____	$_____	$_____	$_____

EXHIBIT B3. THE CLEVELAND FOUNDATION
PROJECT BUDGET REQUEST, cont'd.

PROJECT EXPENSES

	Percent on Project	Organizational Contribution	Other Funding Sources	Cleveland Foundation Request	Total
Personnel Expenses					
Staff Costs					
Position title					
_____	___%	$_____	$_____	$_____	$_____
_____	___%	$_____	$_____	$_____	$_____
_____	___%	$_____	$_____	$_____	$_____
_____	___%	$_____	$_____	$_____	$_____
Staff Costs Subtotal		$_____	$_____	$_____	$_____
Fringe Benefits (explain in narrative)		$_____	$_____	$_____	$_____
Fringe Benefits Subtotal		$_____	$_____	$_____	$_____
Total Personnel Expenses		$_____	$_____	$_____	$_____
Non-Personnel Expenses					
Contract Services					
Consultants		$_____	$_____	$_____	$_____
Legal services		$_____	$_____	$_____	$_____
Temporary services		$_____	$_____	$_____	$_____
Audit services		$_____	$_____	$_____	$_____
Other (explain in narrative)		$_____	$_____	$_____	$_____
Contract Services Subtotal		$_____	$_____	$_____	$_____
Office Space					
Rent		$_____	$_____	$_____	$_____
Utilities		$_____	$_____	$_____	$_____
Furnishings		$_____	$_____	$_____	$_____
Maintenance		$_____	$_____	$_____	$_____
Insurance		$_____	$_____	$_____	$_____
Other (explain in narrative)		$_____	$_____	$_____	$_____
Office Space Subtotal		$_____	$_____	$_____	$_____
Equipment/Supplies					
Office supplies		$_____	$_____	$_____	$_____
Printing		$_____	$_____	$_____	$_____
Postage and delivery		$_____	$_____	$_____	$_____
Copier rental/supplies		$_____	$_____	$_____	$_____
Telephone/fax (local/long distance)		$_____	$_____	$_____	$_____
Repairs/maintenance		$_____	$_____	$_____	$_____
Computer supplies/maintenance		$_____	$_____	$_____	$_____
Other (explain in narrative)		$_____	$_____	$_____	$_____
Equipment/Supplies Subtotal		$_____	$_____	$_____	$_____

EXHIBIT B3. THE CLEVELAND FOUNDATION
PROJECT BUDGET REQUEST, cont'd.

| | PROJECT EXPENSES (continued) | | | |
	Organizational Contribution	Other Funding Sources	Cleveland Foundation Request	Total
Travel Related Expenses				
Air travel	$_____	$_____	$_____	$_____
Out-of-town expenses	$_____	$_____	$_____	$_____
In-town expenses (parking/mileage)	$_____	$_____	$_____	$_____
Meetings/seminars/conference fees	$_____	$_____	$_____	$_____
Other (explain in narrative)	$_____	$_____	$_____	$_____
Travel Related Expenses Subtotal	$_____	$_____	$_____	$_____
Other				
Indirect cost (explain in narrative)	$_____	$_____	$_____	$_____
_____	$_____	$_____	$_____	$_____
_____	$_____	$_____	$_____	$_____
Other Subtotal	$_____	$_____	$_____	$_____
Total Non-Personnel Expenses	$_____	$_____	$_____	$_____
TOTAL PROJECT EXPENSES	$_____	$_____	$_____	$_____

Requesting Organization: _____

Prepared By: _____

Phone Number: _____

EXHIBIT B.4. SUMMARY OF CLEVELAND FOUNDATION REQUEST.

Requesting Organization: _____

Project Title: _____

Expenses	Foundation Request
YEAR 1	
Personnel Expenses	
Staff Costs	$_____
Fringe Benefits	$_____
Personnel Expenses Subtotal	$_____
Non-Personnel Expenses	
Contract Services	$_____
Office Space	$_____
Equipment/Supplies	$_____
Travel/Related Expenses	$_____
Other	$_____
Non-Personnel Expenses Subtotal	$_____
Project Total—Year 1	$_____
YEAR 2	
Personnel Expenses	
Staff Costs	$_____
Fringe Benefits	$_____
Personnel Expenses Subtotal	$_____
Non-Personnel Expenses	
Contract Services	$_____
Office Space	$_____
Equipment/Supplies	$_____
Travel/Related Expenses	$_____
Other	$_____
Non-Personnel Expenses Subtotal	$_____
Project Total—Year 2	$_____
YEAR 3	
Personnel Expenses	
Staff Costs	$_____
Fringe Benefits	$_____
Personnel Expenses Subtotal	$_____
Non-Personnel Expenses	
Contract Services	$_____
Office Space	$_____
Equipment/Supplies	$_____
Travel/Related Expenses	$_____
Other	$_____
Non-Personnel Expenses Subtotal	$_____
Project Total—Year 3	$_____
PROJECT TOTAL	$_____

EXHIBIT B.5. PROJECT BUDGET NARRATIVE.

Please provide a detailed explanation below of items for which you are requesting Cleveland Foundation support. This narrative should accompany the project budget form. Use additional pages if needed.

Requesting Organization:_____

Project Title:_____

Project Duration: From _____ To _____

Line Item   **Explanation**

EXHIBIT B6. THE CLEVELAND FOUNDATION
CAPITAL BUDGET PREPARATION GUIDELINES.

OVERVIEW

Two important components of your grant application are a line-item budget and budget narrative. Please follow the guidelines below carefully.

LINE-ITEM BUDGET

- The line-item budget form should include revenues and expenses associated with the proposed project.
- Revenues should be categorized as committed or anticipated.
- Please include a list of individual donors along with corporate and other foundation support as part of the budget narrative.
- Please **type** all information on the forms.
- Each budget form should include the name of a contact person familiar with the capital budget.

BUDGET NARRATIVE

- The budget narrative should include an explanation of every line item for which you are requesting Foundation support. Examples of how information should be provided follow.

  Fifth Floor Renovation: Costs for renovation of the fifth floor program space will cover the demolition of existing rooms and the creation of new student learning stations. Bids from three contractors averaged $2,000 for the entire job.

  Architect's Fees: The architectural fee is 7.25 percent of the total costs of the project, estimated at $1.3 million. The architect's estimates include such infrastructure costs as HVAC, plumbing, electrical and elevator construction.

EXHIBIT B.7. THE CLEVELAND FOUNDATION CAPITAL BUDGET REQUEST.

Requesting Organization: _____

Project Title: _____

Project Duration: From _____ **To** _____

PROJECT REVENUES

Revenues	Committed	Anticipated	Total Project Revenues
Grants and other support			
Government	$_____	$_____	$_____
Foundations and Corporations			
The Cleveland Foundation	$_____	$_____	$_____
_____	$_____	$_____	$_____
_____	$_____	$_____	$_____
_____	$_____	$_____	$_____
_____	$_____	$_____	$_____
Organizational Income	$_____	$_____	$_____
Bonds	$_____	$_____	$_____
Loans	$_____	$_____	$_____
Individual Donors	$_____	$_____	$_____
Board Members	$_____	$_____	$_____
Bequests	$_____	$_____	$_____
Other	$_____	$_____	$_____
Total Project Revenues	$_____	$_____	$_____
In-Kind (not included in total)	$_____	$_____	$_____

PROJECT EXPENSES

Expenses	Total Project Expenses	Foundation Request
Acquisition Expenses	$_____	$_____
Land Costs	$_____	$_____
Building Costs	$_____	$_____
Other Acquisition Costs	$_____	$_____
Acquisition Expenses Subtotal	$_____	$_____
Construction Expenses	$_____	$_____
Basic Construction/Renovation Costs	$_____	$_____
Fees	$_____	$_____
Equipment	$_____	$_____
Other Construction Costs	$_____	$_____
Construction Expenses Subtotal	$_____	$_____
Total Project Expenses	$_____	$_____

EXHIBIT B.8. CAPITAL BUDGET NARRATIVE.

Please provide a detailed explanation below of items for which you are requesting Cleveland Foundation support. This narrative should accompany the capital budget form. Use additional pages if needed.

Requesting Organization:_____

Project Title:_____

Project Duration: From _____ **To** _____

Line Item   **Explanation**

NOTES

Preface

1. Che Guevara, *Guerrilla Warfare*. Lincoln: University of Nebraska Press, 1985, p. 155.
2. Mao Tse-tung, *Basic Tactics* (Stuart R. Schram, trans.). New York: Praeger, 1966, p. 132.

Chapter One

1. Only recently have scholars begun studying donor motivation. One of the more useful typologies is the one developed by Russ Alan Prince and Karen Maru File, who describe seven distinct donor "personalities" or sets of motivations, in *The Seven Faces of Philanthropy* (San Francisco: Jossey-Bass, 1994). For other insights into donor motivation, I refer you to the works of Paul Schervish, Joseph Mixer, Teresa Odendahl, Jerrold Panas, and Virginia Hodgkinson.
2. "Tax-Exempt Organizations Registered with the IRS," *Chronicle of Philanthropy*, October 3, 1996, p. 42.
3. Loren Renz and Steven Lawrence, *Foundation Giving: Yearbook of Facts and Figures on Private, Corporate and Community Foundations, 1993 Edition*. New York: The Foundation Center, 1994, pp. 31–32.
4. Guevara, *Guerrilla Warfare*, p. 50.

Chapter Two

1. For an excellent discussion of "means and ends," see John Carver, *Boards That Make a Difference*, pp. 56–82 (San Francisco: Jossey-Bass, 1990).

Chapter Four

1. In the notes to Chapter Two, we referred to the concept of ends and means in John Carver's Policy Governance model. For Carver, *ends* are those aspects of an organization's mission that answer the questions: "What good shall we do? For what people? At what cost?" Answering these helps you to clarify your organization's core values and thus identify appropriate funding partners.
2. Niccolò Machiavelli, *The Prince* (Luigi Ricci, trans.). New York: New American Library, 1952, p. 53.

Chapter Five

1. William Mengerink, "The Zen of Grantsmanship." In *Hand in Hand: Funding Strategies for Human Service Agencies*. Rockville, Md.: Fund Raising Institute, 1992, pp.41–56.

Chapter Six

1. Mao, *Basic Tactics*, p. 91.
2. Guevara, *Guerrilla Warfare*, p. 90.
3. Mao, *Basic Tactics*, p. 126.

Chapter Seven

1. James Boswell, *Life of Johnson: A Johnson Reader* (E. L. McAdam Jr. and George Milne, eds.). New York: Pantheon Books, 1964, p. 449.
2. C. Edward Murphy (ed.), *Guide to U.S. Foundations, Their Trustees, Officers and Donors*. New York: The Foundation Center, 1995, Vol. 1, p. vii; L. Victoria Hall (ed.), *Foundation Grants to Individuals*, 9th ed. New York: The Foundation Center, 1995, p. vii.
3. Used by permission of Dr. Susan N. Lajoie, associate director, The Cleveland Foundation.
4. Blaise Pascal, Provincial Letter Number 16. In *Provincial Letters: Pensées*. New York: Penguin Classics, p. 257.

Chapter Nine

1. Burston-Marsteller, 1981. Cited in Bob Smucker, *The Nonprofit Lobbying Guide: Advocating Your Cause—and Getting Results*. San Francisco: Jossey-Bass, 1991, p. 36.
2. *Giving USA*, American Association of Fund-Raising Counsel, 1995, cited in *Chronicle of Philanthropy*, June 1, 1995, p. 19.
3. The Foundation Center, *Foundation Directory*. New York: The Foundation Center, published annually.
4. Robert Wilson (ed.), *American Lobbyists Directory*. Detroit: Gale Research, 1990.
5. A. C. Close (ed.) and others, *Washington Representatives, 1995*. Washington, D.C.: Columbia Books, 1995.

INDEX

A

Access, to grantmakers, 15–18
Advocacy, 114
Advocates: activities for, 122–124; communicating with, 119–121; "gorilla," 118; hiring, 124–125; motivating, 121–122; natural, 116–117; recruiting, 116–119
Agenda, for site visits, 109–112
American Association of Fund-Raising Counsel (AAFRC), consultant information from, 27–28
American Lobbyists Directory, 124
Area of interest, as grant criterion, 30
Asking for support, of friends and family, 36
Asprey, Robert B., 126
Attitude, 73–74
Authority, of grantmakers, 13–15

B

Board members, 36, 69, 109
Broad agency announcement (BAA), 24–25; deciding whether to respond to, 33–34
Budgets: example of drafting, 92–97, 98; follow-up questions on, 103–104; guidelines for preparing, 90–92, 150–159; narrative accompanying, 97, 150, 157

C

Capital funding, 31
Certified fundraising executive (CFRE), 28
Charities, number of, 9
Chief executive officer, 38, 68, 107, 109
The Cleveland Foundation, 10; budget guidelines of, 150–159; proposal guidelines of, 83
Clout, 117–118
Cold call, 46
Collaboration, 85–86, 107
Colleagues, participating and service, 88
Community foundations, 9–10, 122

Concept paper, 61–63, 66
Consultants: for access to grantmakers, 17–18; certified, 28; for influencing advocates, 124–125; for prospect research, 27–28
Corporate executives, as advocates, 121–122
Corporate foundations, 9, 121–122
Credibility, 52–53
Customers, of nonprofits, 6–10

D

Deadlines, for proposals, 102
Developing new project, service, or organization, 20, 21–22; initial phone call when, 48–51; planning approach when, 36–37, 39–40, 42–43
Development officer, 69
Direct access, 15–17
Direct authority, 13, 14
Documents. *See* Preliminary documents; Proposals
Donors, 8

Donors Forum of Chicago Library, 27
Dress, for meetings, 71–72

E

Elected officials, as advocates, 121
Endowment funding, 30
Evaluation: follow-up questions on,
     104; plans for, in proposal, 83,
     97, 99
Executive summary: for advocates,
     120; with proposal, 100

F

Fact sheet, 41; for initial phone call,
     47, 48
Family foundations, 9
Family relationship, 14
Financial information: for advo-
     cates, 120; in proposal, 83,
     89–97, 98
Foundation Center: cooperating
     collections, 131–148; and
     do-it-yourself research, 26–27;
     funding information centers,
     129–148; paid research by, 27;
     reference collections, 130
Foundations: executives of, as advo-
     cates, 122; kinds of, 9–10; num-
     ber of, 9; people associated
     with, 31–33; personal approach
     to, 38–39
Friends and family, 36, 38
Funding: diverse sources of, 12;
     interim and partial, 11–12;
     types of, 30–31
Funding relationship, 5–6, 11–13
Fundraising, 1, 4

G

Gantt chart, 89
Garrett, Milton, 113
"Gorilla grants," 118
Government agencies: approach to,
     38; deadlines of, 102; deciding
     whether to apply to, 33–34; as
     grantmakers, 10; and lobbyists,
     124–125; natural advocates to,
     116–117; requirements of, 79

Grantmakers: access to, 15–18; au-
     thority of, 13–15; as customers,
     6, 9–10; decision making by,
     115; grant criteria of, 29–31;
     people associated with, 31–33;
     priorities of, 13; relationship
     between grantseekers and,
     xiv-xvi, 5–6, 44–45, 73–74;
     showing deference to, 10–11.
     See also Foundations; Govern-
     ment agencies
Grantmakers seeking projects, 20,
     21, 24–26; general preparations
     when, 40–41; initial phone call
     when, 51–52; planning ap-
     proach when, 44; prospect
     research when, 33–34
Grants: gorilla, 118; as interim and
     partial funding, 11–12
Grantseekers: deference shown
     by, 10–11; guerrilla, 126–127;
     prospect research by, 26–34; re-
     lationship between grantmakers
     and, xiv-xvi, 5–6, 44–45, 73–74;
     success rate of, 3. *See also* Non-
     profits
Grantseekers seeking support,
     20–24; general preparations
     when, 35–40, 41–44; initial
     phone call when, 48–51; plan-
     ning approach when, 41–44;
     prospect research when, 26–33
Grantseeking: fundamentals of, 4;
     gaining experience in, 56; guer-
     rilla warfare metaphor for, xiv,
     1–2, 3–4; relationship model
     of, 2; types of transactions in,
     20–21
Guevara, Che, xiv, 18, 56, 57, 66,
     72, 77, 78, 114, 127

I

Implementation plan: follow-up
     questions on, 104; in proposal,
     83, 86–89
Indirect access, 17
Indirect authority, 14–15
Individual foundations, 9
Initial phone call, 46–56; explicit
     messages in, 47, 48–52; implicit

messages in, 47, 52–54; ob-
     jectives of, 47; placing, 47–48;
     setting up meeting in, 47,
     54–56
Institute for Government Public
     Information, 120
Internal Revenue Service (IRS):
     and corporate philanthropy,
     121–122; tax-exempt status
     from, 82
Introductions: in initial phone call,
     41–42; in preliminary meetings,
     74–75

L

Legislators, 8–9, 120–121
Letter: cover, with proposal,
     100–101; as preliminary docu-
     ment, 59–60, 66; of support,
     85, 101–102
Lobbyists, 124–125
Location, as grant criterion,
     29–30

M

Machiavelli, Niccolò, 56
Mao Tse-tung, xiv, 5, 34, 70, 102,
     103
McCormack, Elizabeth, xv
Meeting emergency need, 20,
     22–23; planning approach
     when, 37, 40, 43
Meeting ongoing need, 20, 23–24,
     31; planning approach when,
     37–38, 40, 43–44
Meetings: with advocates, 120; after
     submitting proposal, 103–108;
     dress for, 71–72; during site vis-
     its, 108–113; get-acquainted,
     55–56, 74–76; get-down-to-
     business, 56, 76–77; messages
     to convey in, 104–107; prelim-
     inary, 67–77; setting up, 47,
     54–56
Mengerink, William, 63
Mission: customers related to, 6–7;
     grantseeker's, and grantmaker's
     goal, 25; researching grant-
     maker's, 21

N

National Endowment for the
Arts, 10
National Endowment for the
Humanities, 10
National Society of Fund-Raising
Executives (NSFRE), consultant
information from, 27, 28
Needs: defining, 28–33; statement
of, 104; of those you serve,
20–21. *See also* Meeting emer-
gency need; Meeting ongoing
need
Newspaper articles, 120
Nonprofits: background on, in
proposal, 84–86; customers
of, 6–10; introducing, 41–42.
See also Grantseekers

O

O'Neill, Bard E., 35, 113
Operating support, 31. *See also*
Meeting ongoing need
Organizations. *See* Developing new
project, service, or organization;
Nonprofits
Organizations seeking support. *See*
Grantseekers seeking support

P

Paid access, 17–18
Preliminary documents, 57–66;
concept paper, 61–63; letter,
59–60; white paper, 63–66
Preliminary meetings, 67–77; dress
for, 71–72; get-acquainted,
55–56, 74–76; get-down-to-
business, 56, 76–77; planning
presentation for, 70–71; rehearsals for, 72–74; seating
arrangement for, 72; selecting
participants for, 68–70; setting
up, 47, 54–56; visual aids for, 71
Professional relationship, 14
Program, defined, 22

Program funding, 31
Program officers, 14
Project: continuation of, 83, 99; defined, 22; description of, in proposal, 83, 99; evaluation of, 83,
97, 99, 104; sculpting, 81–82.
See also Developing new project,
service, or organization
Project director, 68–69, 109
Project evaluation and review technique (PERT) chart, 89
Project funding, 30
Proposals, 2; allocating resources
for preparing, 87–89; benefits of
preparing, 88–89, 102; chronol-
ogy for preparing, 84; cover
letter with, 100–101; deciding
whether to submit, 79–81; and
eligibility criteria, 82; evaluation
plans in, 83, 97, 99; executive
summary with, 100; financial
information in, 83, 89–97, 98;
guidelines for, 82–83; implementation plan in, 83, 86–89;
letters of support with, 101–
102; myths about, 78, 79; organization background in, 83,
84–86; project continuation in,
83, 99; project description in,
83, 99; sculpting project for,
81–82; sending, 102. *See also*
Preliminary documents
Prospect research: defining needs
before, 28–31; do-it-yourself,
26–27; identifying individuals
relevant to, 31–33; purchasing,
27–28; when grantmaker seeks
projects, 33–34
Proxy, authority of, 14–15
Purchasing decision makers, as
customers, 7

R

Relationship: family, 14; funding,
5–6, 11–13; professional, 14
Relationship model, of grantseeking, 2

Request for proposals (RFP),
24–25; deciding whether to
respond to, 33–34; initial phone
call responding to, 51–52
Research. *See* Prospect research

S

Sculpting your project, 81–82
Section 501(c)(3), 82
Service. *See* Developing new project,
service, or organization
Site visits, 108–113; agenda for,
109–112; communication be-
fore and after, 112–113; select-
ing participants for, 109
Skloot, Edward, xv-xvi
Solicitation team, 38
Start-up costs, 22
Statement of need, 104
Support: asking for, 36; letters
of, 101–102; type of, as grant
criterion, 30–31

T

Tax-exempt status, 82
Telephone call. *See* Initial phone call
Thayer, Charles W., 46, 67, 125
Timeline matrix, 86–87, 88, 89

V

Videotape, for meetings, 71
Visual aids, for meetings, 71
Voice or tone, of preliminary docu-
ments, 60, 63, 65–66
Volunteer leaders, 69, 75, 107, 109

W

Warm call, 46
Washington Representatives, 124–125
White paper, 63–66
Wolf, Sharon, 1
Written documents. *See* Preliminary
documents; Proposals
Wylie, Joseph C., 19